THE ART OF CALM

Other Books by Brian Luke Seaward

Stressed Is Desserts Spelled Backward:
Rising Above Life's Challenges Through Humor,
Hope, and Courage

Stand Like Mountain, Flow Like Water:
Reflections on Stress and Human Spirituality

Table for Two, Please:
Morsels of Inspiration Over the Noon Hour

Health and Wellness Journal Workbook

Managing Stress:
Principles and Strategies for Health and Wellbeing

Managing Stress:
A Creative Journal

For
my sister Leslie,
may you come to know peace in your heart,
and
for my college buddies, Tom Sarson and Rich Riker,
from our days at the University of Maine—
Remember! "You must relax, or else it will. . . ."
and
for my great friend, Skylar Sherman,
who knows how calming a good laugh really can be!

Contents

Mirrored Stillness • The Candle Flame • Natural Fireworks • Far from the Maddening Crowd • The Healing Power of Blue • Bird on a Wing • Spring to Life • Memory Lane • Thinking Is the Fastest Way to Travel • Bigger Than Life • A Slow Walk in the Woods • Up on the Roof • Under the Sea • Feathers and Grace • A Thousand Shimmering Lights • Windows of the Soul • Laughter in the Aisles • Nature's Way • Paris in Springtime • The Mind's Eye • Quarter Moon in a Ten-Cent Town • A Sunday Drive • Space: The Next Frontier • Alone on the Green • Cathedral Heights • Lunch with Picasso, O'Keeffe and Rembrandt

Relaxing Through the Sense of Sound

Relaxing Through the Sense of Smell

• A River Runs Through It, Really! • Try Turning the TV Off Tonight • The One That Got Away • From a Trot to a Gallop • It's Positively Grand! • Grab Your Helmet and Go • The Blue Lagoon

Acknowledgments

*M*any many thanks go to Peter Vegso, standing at the helm of Health Communications, Inc., who knows a great idea when he sees one. Calm *is* good! Thanks for giving me the opportunity to be part of this new series. Thanks also go to my agent, Tom Grady, and my literary assistant, Susan Griffin. I am ever so grateful to Christine Belleris, Allison Janse, Maria Konicki, Lawna Oldfield, Kim Weiss, Randee Feldman, Kelly Johnson Maragni, Jane Barone, Irena Xanthos, Lori Golden, Lorrie Keip, Suzanne Smith and everyone else at Health Communications, Inc., for all their support. Special words of thanks go to Sandy Wendel, too!

A very gracious thank you goes to my students and workshop participants who offered contributions to this effort. Thanks once again to my wonderful network of family and friends across the country: Laurie and Joe Guiles, Donna and Scott Mefford, Gail and Dwane

Wall, Mary Jane and John Mees, Noell and Mike Pennington, Rob Sleamaker, Jon Robison, Scott Poland, Dan Ault, Dan Sebranek, Jack Boyd (for the new house), Erik Nelson, Gianni Scozarro (for the Discovery connection), and Suzanne and Phil Brink—you guys are the best! Thanks to the inventors of the Apple Powerbook, on which this book was entirely written (relaxing by a fire in the living room, on the back porch or in bed with my dog, Shasta, by my side). Last but not least, thanks to the Source of all creation who, by no surprise, is also the source of all relaxation. Peace!

Introduction:
Please, Come Back to Your Senses

Today in America, the pace of life can best be described as "warp speed." Some might say it's even out of control. Twelve- to fourteen-hour workdays, cellular phones attached to the ear, a barrage of e-mails, multiple voicemail messages, fifty-seven cable channels, Saturday morning soccer games and mandatory office parties—the list goes on and on. While the human condition thrives on mental stimulation, it also requires relaxation, a state of calm. Balance is the key to life.

It wasn't long ago when Sunday was revered by almost everyone as a day of rest and relaxation. Stores were closed on Sunday. Families typically got together and had a big afternoon or evening meal, after which the day would come to an end with song, music or dance. Other days of the week also lent themselves to periods of relaxation as well, particularly the early mornings or evenings after work. It was not uncommon to find people out fishing, curled up with a good book, practicing a musical instrument, or perhaps sewing or knitting around a fire while telling stories to the children. These were the days before television, radio and the World Wide Web. These were simple, perhaps less sophisticated times. With simplicity comes balance. With balance, calm.

Relaxation isn't a science, it's an art. Relaxation is the practice of being calm. It's the practice of staying centered and grounded. Some would contend, it is the art of living in the present moment: To be here now. To be calm, some say, is "to be," rather than "to do." Still others would call this the practice of *mindfulness*.

Cultivating our skills to bring balance into our lives through relaxation is not only enjoyable, it's essential for a healthy life. Sad to say, many people have forgotten how. Current studies reveal what common sense has stated for decades: a fast-track lifestyle without adequate time for rest and relaxation can lead to burnout and chronic illness (*dis*-ease).

With so much focus on stress these days, it seems rather appropriate to place some much-needed attention on the concept of relaxation, the lost art of calm. The art of calm invites us to fully live in the present moment, without judgment or analysis of what we do, or about whom we are with.

Those familiar with the stress response—a heightened state of physical readiness—will tell you that the mind spins into overdrive by perpetually gathering information through our five senses and processes that information into our lives with our thoughts and actions. Interestingly, the same means to sound the stress alarm can be used to deactivate the stress alarm—by redirecting the five senses to focus on various stimuli that promote relaxation.

To smell the freshness of spring air, to taste the texture of ripe strawberries or to hear the rich fullness of a chamber orchestra playing Mozart's *Eine Kleine Nachmusik* on a summer evening—these only begin to describe what the awareness of calming stimuli can do to calm the body.

As a college professor and workshop facilitator in stress management,

I teach scores of people about the art of relaxation. I help them train their minds to access and utilize the energy of the five senses: sight, sound, smell, taste and touch. I also add a sixth dimension that can best be described as the divine sense. The divine mystical aspect includes the awareness of experiences, which combine several of the senses but, perhaps equally so, reach beyond the five senses to give an appreciation that all life is sacred and that we are all the richer for it. Not only are these experiences beyond the five senses, many times they are often beyond words.

In the course of a normal day, our five senses are finely tuned for stimulation—most likely on the lookout for possible stressors. The art of calm allows us to reprogram these same senses to promote a greater sense of relaxation. Some sensual experiences may only last seconds, while others (like a massage) may require a full hour. Herein lies the power of balance—to reach a point of stimulation without becoming overwhelmed by it.

It is fair to say that, for the most part, we have lost touch with the calming power of our five senses. Advances in technology have allowed us to extend our five senses (through microscopes and portable speakers, for example), but in doing so, we have compromised and dulled the intake of calming perceptions through sight, sound, taste, touch and, perhaps most of all, smell.

The art of calm is profound in both depth and scope. The impact of some activities, which may last no longer than a few seconds, begins to redirect the body to homeostasis (a physical calm). You may choose to indulge in other pleasures, such as soaking in a Jacuzzi, for a much longer time period. The end result is the same—a profound state of calm. There is no one way to enter this calming presence. There are hundreds, if not thousands of experiences to promote and produce calmness. The greater our receptivity (and repertoire of choices), the more full our life journey becomes.

This book offers many ideas, suggestions and reminders on how we can reacquaint ourselves with the essence of the sensual aspects of being human. There are twenty-six entries per sense: one for every day of the week (except Sundays) for one month. Some passages may seen like clichés, but remember, clichés are based on simple truths tested through the ages. Relaxation is an individual matter. Not every technique is going to work for you.

As one friend told me as she read this manuscript, "I can imagine meeting God at the gates of heaven, and as we greet each other, he pulls out this list on a clipboard and says, 'Now, let's review what you experienced while on Earth.' I can imagine him saying these are requirements for being human."

Let these ideas germinate and take root in your mind. May these passages and insights remind you regularly to seek balance in your life and live life to the fullest.

Brian Luke Seaward
Boulder, Colorado

ONE

Relaxing Through the Sense of Sight

By our very nature we rely most heavily on the sense of sight. Some estimates suggest we take in 70 percent of our sensory information through the eyes, leaving the remaining 30 percent to the other four senses. If we only had the sense of vision to enjoy the world, we would never cease to be amazed at all the beauty we could find. Colors, patterns, shapes all lend themselves to a banquet of visual sensations, a feast for the eyes. Familiar images bring comfort. New images bring exhilaration from the rapture they provide.

Sometimes we can become overwhelmed by all we take in through our eyes, especially with the advent of computer screens. Too much of anything can lead to sensory overload. Balance is essential. For those times when the view from your office or living room offers no escape, close your eyes and travel on the magic carpet of your imagination to mystical lands, magical scenes and pristine vistas where the views take your breath away and give back your soul.

Beauty may be in the eyes of the beholder, but calmness is in the heart of the individual, and from here it begins to permeate every cell in the body. When beauty is combined with stillness, it is an unbeatable combination for inner peace. Perhaps this is why ocean resorts and mountain cabins are two of the most popular destinations for vacations.

Mental imagery and guided visualization have long been known to create a sense of calm and inner peace. They are also known for restoring a sense of wholeness, which augments the healing process, whether it be due to illness, grief from a significant loss or simply the stress of a hectic day.

In the theme of balance, shouldn't we make an effort to draw into our field of vision an equal amount of those things that calm the nerves? Too many numbers, too many words, too many computer screens tend to overwhelm our brains. This visual noise needs to be balanced.

Years ago, Louis Armstrong once described through imagery all this and more in a song entitled, *What a Wonderful World.* And boy, is it ever!

Mirrored Stillness

Should you happen to come across a small pond in the early morning before the sun's heat tends to kick up the winds, you may notice something special. Naturalists refer to it as mirrored stillness—water so calm that it reflects the trees, the sky, the clouds and all that is around the shores. The corresponding metaphor is that our bodies are like ponds. When we look at a still body of water, the image of calm settles into our unconscious and in turn promotes a deep sense of relaxation. If you cannot get out to a pond or pool of water, bring an image of one to your mind.

The Candle Flame

I f you find yourself stressed at home, take a moment and light a candle, any candle. Once it is lit, sit for a moment and stare at the flame. Observe its shape. Describe the shape from top to bottom. How short or tall is the flame? Now take a slow, deep breath. Next, look closely at the colors. What colors do you see? Once again, take a very slow, deep breath. Next look at the movement of the flame. Is it still? Does the flame dance? How would you best describe the flame's movements? Once again take a very slow, deep breath and relax. If your mind happens to wander, and most likely it will, bring your attention back to the candle's flame. Take another slow, comfortable, deep breath and relax.

Natural Fireworks

SIGHT · SIGHT · SIGHT · SIGHT · SIGHT · SIGHT · SIGHT · SIGHT · SIGHT · SIGHT · SIGHT

The night sky holds many wonders for the eyes to gaze upon. Three of my favorites include these natural fireworks, all of which provide a deep sense of calm.

When I first saw the northern lights, also known as the aurora borealis, I thought someone in town was playing with a spotlight. Then I realized that no person could pull off this show. Upon the night sky was a myriad of magnificent colors dancing in a blaze of patterns: reds, blues, oranges and greens. Words cannot explain the beauty of the northern lights or the sense of awe that nature's fireworks instill in the human spirit. The northern lights are visible to the northern United States during winter and, on rare occasions, spring and fall. Check it out.

Summer thunderstorms also provide a natural light show with an incredible soundtrack. My favorite light show is chain lightning, where the whole sky fires up with several veins of light.

More subtle yet incredibly majestic is a night of falling stars. One shooting star can steal your breath away. You can see these any time of year.

Steal away into the night and watch some natural fireworks. The night sky is filled with tremendous awe.

Far from the Maddening Crowd

Don't you just love to watch people? Not one or two people, but hundreds of people. Like ants. Everyone going in a thousand different directions at the same time, looking busy, some talking, some holding hands, some with headphones. On the surface, it looks like chaos, but there is an order to it all, as each person takes responsibility for him- or herself.

Airports, train stations, shopping malls, busy streets. These are typically places where a critical mass of people is hurrying and scurrying, more often than not stressed about something. But when you sit back and watch the flow of traffic, the faces, the clothes, the interactions, the energy, and realize that you are not part of the rush, it calms the heart muscle.

So here is your next homework assignment. The next time you're in a crowd of people, and you are feeling boxed in, sit down and just watch the flow of human motion. Pay attention to your posture, your breathing and your own energy levels. You will be amazed.

The Healing Power of Blue

C olors have an incredible effect on our emotions and the unconscious feelings that are associated with them. The colors red and orange excite; whereas, the colors blue and some greens are more passive. Feeling blue has nothing to do with seeing blue. Rather, seeing blue—blue skies, blue water, blue flowers— tends to instill a sense of calm. Light therapy is based on this concept in which each color holds a specific vibration. In the spectrum of light therapy, blue is a healing color. So if you find yourself stressed, put on a blue shirt, blouse, T-shirt, jeans or anything that brings the color blue close to your body, and let the healing power begin.

Bird on a Wing

Thousands of Canadian geese have crossed the border and taken permanent residence in a great many states, while others simply head south for the winter months. To see several hundred of these honkers take wing is an incredible sight. Falcons, hawks and eagles in flight are a spectacular sight as well, and to see them hang in the air catching the wind of a thermal draft is inspiring. Seagulls and pelicans offer a similar spectacle, particularly when they seem to glide effortlessly on the breeze of an ocean updraft. Although earth-bound, we can certainly let these winged creatures lift our spirits.

Here is an assignment. Find a place where birds take flight. Sit for a half-hour and do nothing more than watch these marvelous winged creatures in their natural state, and let your spirits soar.

Spring to Life

Spring—a time of renewal. Symbolically a time of birth and newness, like a green shoot sprouting from the ground.

The stress of life often brings with it periods of dying expectations and grieving. Spring and the new growth that comes from the trees, plants and wildlife is a message to put the grieving behind and move on, to spring to life.

So what do you do when you are trying to get out of the grieving process and have passed out of the cycle of spring? The answer is easy. Go to the nearest greenhouse, walk the aisles and observe the new growth. In the realization that all things connect, we, too, have a part of us that yearns for new growth, a part of us that is springing to life. Greenhouse therapy. Won't you give it a try?

13

Memory Lane

The good old days. Those were the days when life was trouble-free and all problems were resolved (well almost). Even if things weren't quite how we remember them, flipping through old photographs can bring back some great memories and with them heartfelt smiles and warm fuzzies. Okay! It's time to look at family photos. So pull out the photo albums and scrapbooks and begin to turn the pages. It does a heart good to remember the good times. As a follow-up, pull together any lingering photos and items that have not made it into a scrapbook. While you are arranging and pasting, think up funny captions for those people who can't share the memory, but who can share in a good laugh or two.

Thinking Is the Fastest Way to Travel

SIGHT · SIGHT · SIGHT · SIGHT · SIGHT · SIGHT · SIGHT · SIGHT · SIGHT · SIGHT · SIGHT

Picture sitting on the steps of Machu Picchu at high noon, or dangling your feet in the pool of the Taj Mahal or walking alone on the beach at Martha's Vineyard at sunset. It doesn't take long to get to a place of comfort when we use our imagination; it happens instantaneously. As a child, you may have been reprimanded in grade school for daydreaming, but in adulthood the practice is strongly recommended, if for no other reason than to beat the stress of life. The average person needs more than just two weeks of sanctioned vacation per year, to keep sane. So when stress arises, the moment calls for a quick mind trip, a cerebral vacation.

Where do you want to go today? Think of five places, exotic or simplistic, but in lands far, far away. If it helps, buy a travel magazine, cut out a photo and place it on your corkboard to serve as a reminder of your quick mental getaway. Who knows, one day you might go there.

Bigger Than Life

During the Great Depression, people would scrimp and save a nickel just to escape the problems of the world in front of the silver screen. With today's hectic pace, movies continue to serve as cinematic escapism. You buy a ticket, leave your worldly troubles at the box office and step into another world—if only for a few hours.

Movies such as *The English Patient, Dr. Zhivago, Lawrence of Arabia, The Last Emperor* and *Out of Africa* are five examples of escapism with incredible cinematography. Keep your eyes on the lookout for epic movies like these. If you cannot make it to the big screen, add these five movies to your personal video collection. Remember, life is bigger than life when you choose to live it that way.

A Slow Walk in the Woods

SIGHT · SIGHT · SIGHT · SIGHT · SIGHT · SIGHT · SIGHT · SIGHT · SIGHT · SIGHT · SIGHT

I magine the shades of color in a forest. The pale green maples, the dark green pine needles, the emerald green beech trees. And the rays of sunlight create a pale yellow umbrella as they filter through the forest canopy. The brown of the rugged, gnarled oak bark contrasts with the ivy-green mountain laurel and pink-and-white lady slippers as a clear blue sky peeks at intervals anticipating a brilliant orange sunset.

Your walk, cushioned with each step by fallen pine needles, meanders through a gauntlet of towering trees—its canopy of leaves covers your head from sun and rain. Chipmunks, squirrels, finches, chickadees and rabbits scatter as you make your way through the woods. Nature offers a sense of calm, from the trees and flowers, to the ponds and animals. I think there is an inherent trust that peace and calm can be found walking on a path in the woods. Even if you don't live near a forest, most everybody lives near a park and the same calming effect is delivered. When was the last time you went for a walk in the woods? Isn't it time to do it again?

Up on the Roof

The phone has been ringing off the hook. Your e-mail in-box has been declared officially full by your provider, and you don't even want to look at the fax-machine bin. You need a break!

Head outside (you city dwellers), but this time rather than going down, go up—to the roof of your building. (If this isn't possible, extend this break to a lunch hour and find a restaurant with a view.) If you were in a national park, you could find a height to look down from. So in this case, the next best thing is a concrete mountain.

Caught in the thick of responsibilities and deadlines one turns myopic. By getting above the situation, even for a few moments, we tend to put things in perspective and bring reality back in balance. See you up on the roof.

Under the Sea

My angel fish, Raphael, swims so gracefully in my fish tank that I could just sit and watch him for hours. In fact, I do. Studies have shown that people who observe the motions of fish in tanks have lower resting blood pressure and heart rates after viewing these sea creatures than before they started. For people without the means to have their own fish tank, there are even videos to buy of fish swimming in aquariums (I prefer the real thing). Restaurants often use aquariums to instill a sense of peaceful ambiance. Dentists' offices do too.

So here is a homework assignment. Find two restaurants (not dentists' offices) in your town that have large aquariums and take yourself to lunch. And if you should become so inspired, perhaps you might even get a fish tank of your own with an angel fish.

Feathers and Grace

With a beak nearly as long as its legs and a five-foot wing span, the blue heron is the epitome of grace. It moves slowly as it wanders the shore's edge in search of food—occasionally extending its wings, defying gravity, to take flight.

Once I spotted a blue heron across a marsh in southwest Florida. As I pulled out my camera, the heron was startled by a fox and took flight. With its huge gossamer wings beating ever so slowly, it boldly chose a path directly over my head. As I continued to watch the bird gather altitude as it headed to the opposite shore, one of its feathers sailed out from the wing and, in what seemed like minutes, landed softly at my feet. Sometimes the impossible can take wing and fly. Style is grace under pressure.

A Thousand Shimmering Lights

SIGHT · SIGHT · SIGHT · SIGHT · SIGHT · SIGHT · SIGHT · SIGHT · SIGHT · SIGHT · SIGHT

Sometimes the beauty of a place is greatest when we step back from it long enough to see the full perspective. Such is the case with cities, particularly if you can seek a vantage point on high to look down over the entire metropolis. Most often that beauty shines at night when the city lights flicker like stars in the heavens.

Here's an idea. The next time you find there is absolutely nothing to watch on television, or you find that the selection of movies at the cineplex is not hitting your entertainment threshold, take a drive to a point at the edge of town, turn the car around so you are facing the city, then turn the engine off. If the weather is good and you can find a place to sit comfortably in the fresh air, pick a spot. If not, just sit behind the wheel and look below. Gaze upon the sea of lights, a heaven of flickering points of illumination.

23

Windows of the Soul

So often people don't make true eye contact, perhaps out of shyness or fear, maybe annoyance, and some for cultural reasons. But if we really did take the time to look into each other's eyes, without being invasive, we would learn that there is a peace and a beauty within each and every eye we see. Shakespeare once said the eyes are the windows of the soul. To look into the eyes is to see the essence of the human spirit. The next time you talk to someone, gaze gently into his or her eyes and speak to the person's soul. And should you not find a calm presence, share any calmness you can from within yourself.

Laughter in the Aisles

SIGHT · SIGHT · SIGHT · SIGHT · SIGHT · SIGHT · SIGHT · SIGHT · SIGHT · SIGHT · SIGHT

One of my friends has a unique antidote for the blues. When she's feeling down and out, she heads to the nearest card shop for a session of humor therapy. She selects birthday cards, St. Patrick's Day cards, cards for any occasion and reads them, searching for an endorphin rush. Her new favorite cards are the wacky photograph cards with funny expressions. She says cards never fail to lift her spirits.

I went with her once. We were rolling in the aisles with laughter. Now I find myself going to "greeting-card counseling" quite often. It's amazing how inexpensive good therapy really is.

Nature's Way

To see a mountain vista with clear blue skies, to gaze at an ocean beach with palm trees swaying to a calypso wind—these are two of hundreds of ways we reconnect to the natural world. If getting to a peaceful corner of nature is a challenge, bring a piece of nature to your home or office, such as a plant, a seashell or some cut flowers—all of which hold the energy of nature. When you are stressed, gaze upon the leaves of a rhododendron, the barnacles on a seashell or the petals of a flower bouquet. Gaze long enough to get the message to relax.

Paris in Springtime

I have never been to Paris but have always wanted to go. I hear that Paris in springtime is the best—the flowers, the chalk drawings on the sidewalks, the little boys delivering baguettes of bread on their bikes. I can see it all now: the Eiffel Tower, the Champs-Elysées, boats on the Seine, Notre Dame, the Louvre. Ask anyone to name a city that conjures up romance and enchantment, and Paris is at the top of many people's lists, even if, like me, they have never been there.

Cities have an allure that reaches a peak in springtime. Even if it rains, the new leaves on trees, the tulips and daffodils, the pockets of green grass here and there give a sense of life out of the doldrums of winter. Paris is not the only city that has springtime magic, but symbolically it conveys romance, and romance brings peace to the heart. So if you can't make it to Paris, try something closer to home: San

Francisco, Chicago or Boston. The peace of romance is not in the city, it's in the heart of the people who live and visit there. Be spontaneous. Make some reservations today. Bon voyage!

If, however, your schedule is tight, relax! Instead, find a romantic place to stroll in your own city or town—where the trees are blossoming and the robins have returned to signal the start of spring.

The Mind's Eye

Use the power of imagination through your mind's eye to calm the mind and body. For aspiring Buddhists, this idea comes from a few of my students who spent the equivalent of *Seven Years in Tibet* in Boulder. Simply imagine you are viewing yourself as if you have stepped outside the shell of your body and are sitting behind yourself. In this capacity as the observer, you don't judge your thoughts as good or bad, you simply observe them. If this seems difficult at first, then visualize yourself sitting on the bank of a river, and each log that moves down the river is labeled with a thought from your mind. Keep the logs floating until your mind is clear. Only then will you reach the ultimate state of relaxation.

Quarter Moon in a Ten-Cent Town

Do you know what phase the moon is in tonight? Most people don't. First quarter, last quarter or full? Throughout the history of humanity, observing the moon has been a form of meditation. It remains so today.

To see the crescent moon hanging low in the sky at sunset, or perhaps a half moon suspended between Jupiter and Mars, or a full moon at sunrise provides a sense of grounding, a sense of security, for we know that however uncertain some things may be, there is also a level of predictability to life. Aside from the sheer beauty of a heavenly body so close to Earth, observing the moon in all its many phases is a powerful reminder of the phase of our own life cycle.

So go outside tonight and find the moon in the sky; observe it for a few minutes. And every now and then when you find yourself feeling a little off center, look for the moon in the sky and use it as a personal compass to keep yourself grounded.

A Sunday Drive

Years ago, people would get in their cars on a Sunday afternoon and just drive around. That was when gasoline was forty-nine cents a gallon and stores were closed on Sundays. The idea of a Sunday drive is a good one. It gets you out of the house, away from work, and on the weekends when traffic isn't a concern, it gives the mind room to roam, which is always a good thing.

So what are your plans this Sunday? We spend so much travel time in the car, it would be nice to try it without a destination. Got a few extra hours to explore the neighborhood and beyond? Sure you do. Gas up the car and go.

Space: The Next Frontier

Within the next decade, commercial space travel may be as easy as flying from New York to Paris, although most likely a bit more expensive. (How about those frequent flyer miles?) Space travel is appealing to a great many people, if for no other reason than to float around without the tug of gravity as a reminder of our earthly existence. To view our planet from afar, to observe stars and constellations unobstructed by artificial light, to have a front seat at the stage of heaven—what more could you ask for? Until then, the best we can do is lie on a blanket spread on a field of grass and look up to the heavens.

Actually this is a very good way to spend an evening. Of course the farther away from city lights you are, the better the view. August is great to glimpse shooting stars as the Earth moves into the Perseus meteor belt, but falling stars can be found just about any night. The alignment of planets in relation to the lunar cycle is intriguing as well. Pick a constellation, any one will do, and stare at it for several minutes. Take a deep breath and close your eyes. Then open them and find another constellation, breathe again and relax. (If light pollution is a problem in your locale, then the next best thing is a trip to a planetarium.)

Alone on the Green

The first (and last) time I hit a golf ball on a golf course, I struck the windshield of a parked car. Yikes! At that moment I decided to take up jogging instead. But a great many of my friends play golf. I'm told, what begins as a social sport quickly becomes a program in stress management. For some, it's the only time to commune with nature.

Given the bias of these particular golfers, perhaps it was no surprise to hear their choice of a relaxing image—being alone on the green was the unanimous answer. As I listened to them individually describe a perfect Sunday morning, their answers were consistent. They went something like this:

"There I am approaching the eighth hole. The sun's first rays are reaching the treetops. There are three colors visible: green grass, blue skies and a few white puffy clouds. The air is crisp, but not cold.

35

There is not a sound anywhere. Before me at the edge of the fairway are two deer. For the moment, the last thing I am thinking about is a golf ball. I pause and take it all in. This is heaven." So this weekend, set up a tee time for 7:00 A.M.

Cathedral Heights

Have you ever stepped inside a gothic cathedral? Notre Dame, St. John the Divine, The National Cathedral? The grandeur of the structure is almost too much for your eyes to take in—from the vaulted ceiling to the intricate metalwork, the multitude of statues and aging frescoes. Not only are these revered cathedrals bigger than the eye can behold (and, in a way, they are supposed to be), their enormity can dwarf our problems. Amen to that!

In addition to the grandeur of the structure is the brilliance of colors from the stained glass windows—ever changing as the sunlight dances through the day. Most of all is the peace that exudes from each and every corner, an implicit peace that reminds us we are never alone. Next time you happen to drive by a cathedral, make it a point to get out of the car and step inside for a moment. If a cathedral is too far, find the next best thing (a church, temple or other familiar religious wonder).

Lunch with Picasso,
O'Keeffe and Rembrandt

High ceilings, large arches, benches to sit on, open spaces, white walls and great artwork. A temple of sorts. By and large art galleries tend to be rather quiet inside, too. There is a reason for this. When the mind is engaged in appreciation, the mouth falls silent. The noon hour is a popular time to go to museums, if only for a short visit. It offers a chance to sit in a quiet place and enjoy beauty, perhaps even become inspired, but definitely motivated for the rest of the afternoon.

When was the last time you went to an art gallery? When was the last time you ate lunch with Pablo Picasso, Claude Monet, Georgia O'Keeffe, Winslow Homer, Grant Wood or local artists? Gallery boutiques are great places to become inspired by great (or soon-to-be great) works of art.

TWO

Relaxing Through the Sense of Sound

Music, it is said, soothes the savage beast, a fact known and respected in every culture for millennia. From lullabies to George Winston piano solos, music's power to relax is revealed in the subtleties of melody, pitch, timbre, harmony and tone. Good vibrations of any kind disarm the most ardent emotions and transport the human spirit to a place of comfort and joy.

Sound is energy made audible. Physiologically speaking, the nervous system translates the vibrations of sound into pleasant or unpleasant impulses, which either stress or relax the body. Vibrations travel from the ear via the vagus nerve to the brain, and soothing sounds caress the brain to induce a sense of relaxation. What's more, alongside this nerve is a track of the lymphatic system allowing white blood cells of the immune system to pick up the beat and resonate with a healing vibration as they migrate throughout the body as well.

But the eardrum is not the only portal of entry in which sound can enter. As energy, sound can enter the body through the bones and skin too, making for a dynamic receptivity to good vibrations.

Perceptions vary regarding quality of music and sounds. Good sounds we regard as pleasant; disturbing sounds are simply noise. One person's symphony is another person's disturbance. Through it all we know that sounds from music, to bird songs, to ocean waves, have a powerful means to instill a wonderful sense of relaxation.

R_x for Good Vibrations

Good music, really good music, can lift the spirits and launch the soul on calmer waters. Try this: Make a list of your favorite songs or pieces of music, ones that really lift your spirits and fill your heart with joy. Then make a mix of these tracks on a cassette tape or CD (while pre-made mixes are good, it is even better when you are the producer of your own). If you don't happen to have all the music you want, invest in a few CDs or borrow from your friends. Many public libraries loan CDs now as well. Make it a point to listen to your selection when driving or walking or perhaps resting at home after a long day at work. Follow your prescription for music therapy and listen to your selections often.

A Classical Experience

othing is more relaxing than a summer concert under the stars with a full orchestra playing Mozart's *Concerto in C Minor.*

For some, classical music is love at first sound. For others the music of the masters—the likes of Beethoven, Brahms, Tchaikovsky and Chopin—is an acquired taste (usually after years of the monotonous predictability of contemporary pop). This summer, be adventuresome. Get some tickets to the Mozart summer series or the local chamber music festival and hear classical music the way it is meant to be heard—under the stars.

If you wish to conduct your own summer concert at any time, in any setting, I suggest these classical favorites, guaranteed to calm the soul:

A Magical Classical Playbill

- Beethoven's *Fur Elise*
- Faure's *Sicilienne* and *Adante molto moderato* (Opus 80)
- Barber's *Adagio*
- Mendelssohn's *Nocturne* from *A Midsummer Night's Dream*
- Mozart's *Concerto in C Minor*

The Reassuring Voice

Remember those humiliating or horrible moments in our younger days—when life just didn't seem fair? The reassuring voice of a parent or grandparent nurtured our souls. And things weren't so bad after all.

Life still doesn't always seem fair, especially after grueling, stress-filled twelve- to fourteen-hour workdays. That's when it's time for the voice of a good friend to reassure us that we'll get beyond the potholes in life.

So who is that person in your life? Who constitutes your informal support group? Research shows that support groups are crucial for well-being, physically, mentally, emotionally and spiritually. Whose most reassuring voice acts not only as a sounding board, but echoes a sound of stability along the rocky coast of life's journey? Give that person a call just to say hello, and then listen . . . listen to the calming voice of a good friend or family member.

Winds of Change

When I ask my students and workshop participants to name sounds that they find calming, not one semester goes by without someone including the sound of wind through the trees on a spring evening, or the current of air as it passes through the skies, moving clouds from one end of the horizon to the other.

Quite literally, winds of each season cleanse the stagnant air. And although the winds of change may be forceful in their attempt to renew the atmosphere, they also bring about a sense of newness, a clean slate, so to speak.

Metaphorically, winds also bring change. I think the reason why we find the sound of wind whistling through the trees, sweeping across the prairies, breezing down the beach and charging down mountain valleys so calming is that, at a deep level, we know that change is good. A clean slate is always welcome.

45

Step outside and sit quietly for a moment. Listen for the wind. Listen as each breeze that ushers by brings with it a new breath of life.

Three Simple Words

The human voice can be one of the most beautiful sounds in the world. But it's not just the sound that holds the potential to be a calming presence, it's the intention behind the words that carries a message of peace.

The words "I love you" have such an intention. To tell your spouse, child, parent, significant other, friend or pet these words not only sends a vibration of peace between two hearts, it comes back to us in ways we cannot even imagine. The purest intention is unconditional. Say these three words without any expectation that you will get a reciprocal response. Someone needs to hear these three simple words today. Let the search begin.

Laughter Is Still the Best Medicine

SOUND · SOUND · SOUND · SOUND · SOUND · SOUND · SOUND · SOUND · SOUND · SOUND

I t's no secret that adults take themselves too seriously. But research proves my point. Somewhere between adolescence and college graduation, the muscles that contract the funny bone shrivel up. Consider this: On average, a child laughs about 300 to 400 times a day. Adults laugh fewer than 40. It's time to lighten up and start flexing the humor muscle more frequently.

Laughter is contagious. Hearing someone else break into a guffaw can turn a frown into a smile instantly. Research on humor therapy reveals that laughter is indeed good medicine. It lowers resting heart rate, blood pressure and breathing rate, massages internal organs and relieves muscle tension.

So how can you increase your laughter quota? Try to find one humorous thing a day: a child's comments, a funny e-mail or an ironic bit of news. Here's another idea: Create a tickler notebook filled with cards, cartoons—such as my favorite, Calvin & Hobbes—and photographs of things that make you laugh, smile and chuckle till you feel it in your stomach. Ha ha!

Day of the Dolphins

Our planet hums. It's called the Schumman resonance and it's calculated to be 7.83 hz. Ancient mystics and astronomers alike refer to it as "music of the spheres." When astronauts ride the space shuttle out of Earth's gravitational pull, a simulated vibration is emitted within the spacecraft to replicate this resonance, as a means to ensure the health and well-being of the crew.

Perhaps it's no coincidence that dolphin and whale songs also are measured at 7.83 hz—the vibration of homeostasis (or physical calm). Dolphins seem to be wearing a perpetual smile. Perhaps they know that the secret to life hums along at 7.83 hz.

There was a time when only people who lived near the ocean could hear the songs of dolphins. However, through the advances of technology, today you can bring this healing vibration right into your living room via the stereo system. It's not hard to find a CD with the inspiring, yet haunting dolphin songs. Spend a day with the dolphins and hear the music of the spheres.

The Best Acoustic Piano

A friend once commented that if he had one wish, it would be to hire pianist George Winston for the evening to play on his baby grand piano, while he and his wife sat by candle-light. "Wouldn't that be the best?" he dreamed. I have often had the same thought myself, and I don't even own a piano.

When you cannot bring the pianist to the piano, try bringing your ears (and of course the rest of your body) to the pianist. Look in the newspaper for local concerts for an evening of heavenly bliss. When I do, I am never disappointed. Try it sometime.

And for the nights when you feel like having a private concert in your living room where cloud nine awaits you, then these classic acoustic piano CDs are a must. Light a candle, dim the lights, recline on the couch, close your eyes and listen.

Sublime Acoustic Piano Playbill

- David Lanz: *Christofori's Dream*
- Jonathan Cain: *For a Lifetime*
- Robin Spielberg: *In the Arms of the Wind*
- Jim Wilson: *Northern Seascape*
- Danny Wright: *Phantasys*
- Tom Barabas: *Sedona Suite*
- Tian: *Shanghai Dream*
- Yanni: *In My Time*

The First Signs of Spring

I t happens every year. February ends. Yet the official start of spring seems months away. The weather report warns of a doozy of a snowstorm headed your way. In northern climes, when winter seems to drag on forever, take this trip with me:

It's early morning. The sun has just peeked over the horizon. I am outside walking my dog. Within moments, my attention turns to the sound of a bird singing. It can't be, I rationalize—too early. I pass it off as wishful thinking. Then, as I question my eardrums, I hear it again. This time I know what I hear. It's the song of the robin, looking for his mate. It's the laugh of the flicker trying to rendezvous with her lover. It's the unmistakable melody of the wood thrush.

I cannot think of a more beautiful sound than the first bird songs of spring. It always puts a smile on my face and brings a sense of peace to my heart. I know I am not alone.

54

Bird songs are a blessing any time of year. To attract birds to your backyard, consider investing in a bird feeder or birdbath.

The Sounds of Silence

SOUND · SOUND · SOUND · SOUND · SOUND · SOUND · SOUND · SOUND · SOUND · SOUND

There is indeed a time when no sound, no noise, no music, no talking is the preferred choice. Most likely, it's the time when life seems to be going at warp speed, when even the most delicate of sounds crashes in a cacophony of mind-splitting noise. Even the hum of the florescent lights bothers you. All you want is peace and quiet, with an emphasis on the quiet. What you seek are the sounds of silence.

Although some say it is impossible to be in the absence of any noise (we live in a dynamic world), it is possible to create an ambiance of quiet. Find a room in your house where you can sit or lie undisturbed. Unplug the phone, turn off the television and remove the ticking clock and anything else that might be a distraction. Mark your boundaries well. If anyone else is home, announce your intention to be left undisturbed for the next half hour. Then sit still and listen. What you most likely will notice is the sound of your breath—long, slow and deep. And this is all you need to hear.

Angelic Whispers

S omewhere between birth and six years is the age of innocence, when children, yet uncorrupted by commercial consumerism and the onset of raging hormones, provide that levity between calmness and insanity. Hold a child on your lap and listen to her talk. She may ask questions and try to reason with concepts that make no sense, yet she'll try so hard to understand the adult world.

Children look to us for help and, with a wink, we tell them something we think they can grasp. More often than not, they surprise us.

If you're lucky, she may crawl up on your shoulder and whisper a secret in your ear. A sweet soft voice with a pitch of innocence is refreshing. It calls us back to our youth when times were simpler, less complicated and less worrisome. Children may not speak like angels all the time, but there are moments when they do a good job of imitating the source. If it has been years since you heard these angelic whispers, you are long overdue. Consider taking a walk to your nearest park and sitting under a shade tree, listening to the sounds and laughter of children.

A Mother's Voice

 special bond exists between mother and child, a bond unique unto itself. For nine months a child hears his mother's voice as a vibration that transcends the human nervous system. For the next several years, the mother's voice offers security and protection, familiarity and love. So it's not surprising that the voice of one's own mother ranks rather high on the chart of calming sounds among a great many people.

It's a mutual connection, because she finds your voice calming as well. Daughters especially remark how reassuring a mom's voice is during those rites of passage that only a mother can understand. It's a voice of stability, of groundedness, of love.

The role of a mother is not easy. Today would be a good time to call and tell her you love her. Thank her for those times when her reassuring voice was all it took to calm you. Then listen. If your mom has passed on, tell her in a prayer.

Praise Is the Sound Joy Makes

SOUND · SOUND · SOUND · SOUND · SOUND · SOUND · SOUND · SOUND · SOUND · SOUND

A prayer of gratitude is a song of praise and thanksgiving at any time of year. A prayer of gratitude is joy realized. In a state of calm and tranquility, the walls of the ego lower and sometimes disappear. At this point, the veils of illusion are cleared and we see we are always in the presence of the divine. This realization, however we articulate it, is a song of praise to the source of all creation for our humble gratitude. When we offer our voice in praise to God, or to those who represent the works of God, we raise the spirits of all of those around us. The sound of joy reverberates in all directions.

When was the last time you offered praise aloud?

Scotland the Brave

While on holiday in Scotland with my sister Gail, who was celebrating her thirtieth birthday, we took a wrong turn on a road looking for the Loch Ness monster and actually discovered something much more fascinating—a local bagpipe festival. Perhaps the most memorable part was the lone piper in full Scottish regalia playing the national anthem, *Scotland the Brave.* After a full rendition, he was joined by several hundred clansmen for a grand finale. Everyone was moved to tears, including the only two Americans in the bunch. Something in the tone of a bagpipe stirs the soul with a resonance of tearful bliss.

The tail end of our trip brought us to Shannon, Ireland, where we dined at Bunratty Castle our last night abroad. As we walked from the car to the palace entrance, there stood a lone bagpiper playing *Scotland the Brave* once more. Bagpipe music, I was to learn, is not only found in Scotland. It can be heard on every continent.

Now and again, when I hear the faint sound of bagpipes playing in the distance (at college graduations, sporting events, etc.), I am reminded of my trip to the old country of peaceful hills and valleys, big hearts and warm smiles. And once again I am reminded that all is good.

You don't have to go to Scotland to hear the drone of a lone bagpipe. There are several festivals nationwide, or you can purchase CDs of recorded masters and bring the bonny, bonny land to your world.

The Smallest Angels

One day as I sat on the patio, less than three feet from where the hummingbird feeder dangled, filled with clear sweet water, a tiny angel appeared out of nowhere directly in front of me (to be honest, at first I thought it was a huge bee). The hum of the wings was unmistakable. The bird approached and came within inches of my face. The humming pulsated in my ears. Then, in a flash, he darted toward the bird feeder and perched, sucking the secret nectar for several minutes. Then he was gone. Within seconds another hummingbird appeared and repeated the process.

If you don't have a hummingbird feeder, I highly recommend it, for it seems the smallest of birds can relieve the biggest of problems, if only temporarily. What makes the sound of the hummingbird unique is the pitch of the sound of their wings vibrating at an incredible rate. But hummingbirds do more than hum. In an extremely high-pitched voice, they shriek, usually in delight. When you hear this noise, the delight is shared by two.

Trains of Thought

The train was created in a much simpler time when the pace of life was a fraction of what it is now. The symbolism is profound. If you listen closely, there is a consistent, hypnotic rhythm of the wheels as they move across the tracks. Clickety clack, clickety clack, clickety clack.

Repetitive sounds provide a mantra for the mind. The focus of the repeated motion acts like a broom, sweeping the mind clear of unnecessary thoughts that rob the soul of peace. As the train fades from sight and hearing, let the train metaphorically take with it the stressful thoughts that no longer serve you.

For generations, trains have offered a sense of romance and adventure. Where are they going? When will they get there? Who might you meet on a train? Trains still offer that escape. And if you should find yourself at an intersection waiting for a train to pass, rather than getting stressed, roll down your window, close your eyes and let the clickety clack be a mantra for your mind.

An Evening with Frank, Ella and Tony

SOUND · SOUND · SOUND · SOUND · SOUND · SOUND · SOUND · SOUND · SOUND · SOUND

Singing starts and ends with a rattling of the vocal cords. But crooning—well, crooning comes from a deeper softer place, most likely the seat of the soul. Let me explain: Mick Jagger sings, Frank Sinatra croons. Janis Joplin belts, Ella Fitzgerald croons.

While Tony Bennett and the music of the late Frank Sinatra have enjoyed newfound success with Generation X, crooning is a lost art today.

The voices of Frank, Ella and Tony are indeed rare treasures. They sing with a calming vibration that sweeps your cares and worries away. To hear Frank sing *Young at Heart*, Ella sing *Night and Day* or Tony sing just about anything is like taking a nap on a feather bed. It's comforting, it's relaxing and, above all else, it brings a special harmony to mind, body and spirit.

So here's an idea. If you don't already have one, pick up a CD of any one of these three (Nat King Cole is an excellent choice, too!). After dinner, hit the play button and dim the lights. If you like, hum along.

"Night and day, da da da . . ."

A Warm Hearth

The logs are on the fire; the crinkled newspaper sits strategically under each log. The flue is open and a window is cracked somewhere in the house to create a slight draft. You light the match *pssis-hiss*, it goes up in flames, and you carefully reach in to ignite several of the newspapers. The burning sound of papers begins, soon followed by the crackling of wood as the logs catch fire.

Close the screen, dim the lights, crawl up on the couch and snuggle under a blanket. Close your eyes, and listen to the comforting crackling and popping sounds of burning wood. Your mind drifts but quickly returns with the sound of a log falling beneath the grate. You get up slowly and stoke the fire, placing one more log on the remnants of charred wood. As you return to your spot on the couch, you doze off to the sounds of pinewood snapping.

The Sound of a Lone Flute

SOUND · SOUND · SOUND · SOUND · SOUND · SOUND · SOUND · SOUND · SOUND · SOUND

The sound of a lone flute pierces your soul. It finds that hallowed place that seems dormant and awakens it. All other sounds fade into darkness as the light of the lone flute comes forth.

I first heard R. Carlos Nakai a decade ago. He had given a concert in Boulder to a packed house. Carlos is a Native American, a member of the Navajo and Ute tribes. He stood alone on stage for hours, playing a lone flute.

To the uncultured ear, his music was simplistic. To the free spirit, his melodic flute tunes were magical, haunting and spiritual. I was inspired to buy a CD of his music, *Earth Spirit.* I play it in the evenings before I go to sleep. My body floats on a river of lone flute music. Most likely yours will, too!

Chime Right In

On the front range of Colorado, the chinook winds can be fierce. Sometimes the gusts are measured as high as 100 miles per hour. It rattles the windows and doors. It tears off shingles. Anything not nailed down ends up in Kansas or Nebraska.

I received a set of tubular chimes from my sister Leslie and hung it on the back porch.

No matter what the weather, from the clanging to the pinging of aluminum tubes as they gently rub or knock against the wooden plate in the center of the circle, the chimes have always been a source of comfort throughout the day, but particularly as I retire in the evening. My neighbors think so, too. I noticed that soon after I hung my set, a similar set dangled from their porch, but with a different pitch so that the two appeared to be in conversation. Even in the harshest of winds, the chimes kept their cool.

Chimes come in all lengths and respective chord progressions. Try them out sometime and wait for the next breeze.

Distant Thunder

Picture this: It is summertime, early evening. The cloud banks to the west are as black as they are thick. The air is filled with electricity. Then stillness. A flash of light. A clap of thunder in the distance. And within seconds the lights go out.

As a child, you were terrified of the thunder. Your parents calmed you by telling you the angels were bowling. You took relief in their answer. Years later you learned to count the seconds between the flash and the noise. Still, years later the power failure offers a period of relief. In fact, at some level, you welcome the quiet time and the absence of electrical hum throughout the house.

Try this: The next time you feel a charge of electricity preceding a rip-roaring thunderstorm, lie on the couch, or perhaps even your bed. With your head propped up with a pillow, gaze out into the darkness until your eyelids become too heavy. Then give in to the darkness and focus on the sounds of thunder. Under a blanket or a sheet or in the arms of a loved one, take comfort in the stillness, punctuated by natural electrical current, until you fall asleep.

Hiking to the Top of Windham Hill

SOUND · SOUND · SOUND · SOUND · SOUND · SOUND · SOUND · SOUND · SOUND · SOUND

Decades ago two guitarists, William Ackerman and Alex De Grasi, pooled their money and each recorded an album under the label Windham Hill Records, named after a favorite childhood place in Vermont. They invited some friends (Michael Hedges and Liz Story) to join their group creating a maverick sound: solo acoustic music that evokes a sense of nature.

Some called it environmental jazz, others called it New Age, still others called it the best relaxation music ever. Ultimately, the name New Age stuck, despite the fact that founder William Ackerman despises the name. Then George Winston came along with a CD called *December*, and the rest is history.

Although it may be argued that nature already has a perfect soundtrack which cannot be improved upon, to stand atop a hill, mountain or ocean beach listening to a melodic acoustic song via a portable CD or tape player is arguably one of the most euphoric relaxation techniques. If you don't already have a portable sound system, see if you can borrow one and climb to the top of Windham Hill for an incredible view of the acoustic landscape.

An Afternoon in Salzburg

T he hills are still alive with the sound of music in Salzburg, the home of Maria Von Trapp. Like many European cities, Salzburg hosts several churches, each adorned with a tall steeple containing one, if not several, huge bells. At six o'clock in the evening the bells ring, first in one church, then another as if they are members of a choir stationed strategically around the city in a command performance for anyone who could listen. Some bells offer a soft chime, others give a stronger pitch. When I experienced this phenomenon, the sound of one particular bell seemed to reverberate throughout my entire body. It was as if I were living inside a music box, with the music resonating off the mountainsides and echoing back to the center of town.

Everyone (not just tourists) seemed to pause from daily routines and turn their heads toward the sky in acknowledgment of the choir of church bells, a clarion call to stillness. For a brief moment all was still, save the church bells, and it was glorious.

On Sundays in various towns and cities throughout the United States, you can hear the sound of church bells. This sound always transports me to Salzburg. Open your window and listen. Where does the clanging of bells take you?

Ten Thousand Wings

Consider for a moment the gentle sound of butterfly wings in graceful flight from one flower to another. So soft, so delicate, the sound can only be heard in absolute stillness. The wings of a butterfly are barely paper thin. Now imagine if you will, what that sound would be like if five thousand butterflies perched on a large boulder in Mexico, Africa or Madagascar. The sight of migrating monarchs, for example, is truly beautiful, but the sound—a magnificent symphony of ten thousand wings—takes your breath away.

Natural butterfly gardens around the country are host to several hundred butterflies each and every day. If you go, and I highly recommend a visit, listen closely and you can hear the gentle whisper of fluttering wings. Nature's gift is free.

Water, Water Everywhere

The sound of trickling, flowing or rushing water is music to the ears and nothing less than a tranquilizer for the nervous system. Who cannot marvel at the sound of raindrops falling on window panes, or the rhythmic motion of ocean waves pounding the shore, or columns of water cascading hundreds of feet over weathered rocks to a churning pool below, or the dribble of a mountain stream as it gently rolls over rocks and logs, working its way toward the ocean? Listen, where do you hear the sounds of water?

The age of high-tech living has removed us from the natural environment so that natural sounds to calm and relax both mind and body are heard only during vacation retreats, if then. Although not entirely natural, the benefits of technology have allowed for the re-creation of these sounds through marvelous recordings or even indoor waterfalls.

So check your water level. When is the last time you actually listened to the sound of water? If the answer is less than a week, try one of two solutions. Pick up a CD playing variations on these natural sounds or, better yet, create a space in your home for a small fountain.

Nature's Evening Rhapsody

SOUND · SOUND · SOUND · SOUND · SOUND · SOUND · SOUND · SOUND · SOUND · SOUND

There is a time each year, far from the sounds of concrete and cars, where the world of darkness is anything but still. This magical moment occurs early in the summer season when the world at the edge of the city comes alive with sounds. It begins about an hour or two after sunset, when the veil of darkness covers the planet and the movements and calls of all things nocturnal are present. It continues well into the evening.

Open your window, close your eyes and listen closely. First you will notice the sounds of the cicadas as they rub their wings together (nature's first violin). Perhaps you'll hear the chirps of tree frogs as they put out a call looking for a date. Then come the coyotes, singing their solos in harmony. Next on cue, the hoot of the owl.

This is nature's symphony: an evening rhapsody that is a comforting reminder that we are part of the whole.

THREE

Relaxing Through the Sense of Smell

Perhaps there is no quicker way to relax than to smell the fragrance of newly cut long-stemmed roses or the aroma of fresh ground coffee or perhaps the first hint of autumn on the tail of a late summer evening breeze. It is fair to say that our sense of smell is the least used of our five senses. We tend to rely more on our sense of vision and hearing, leaving the sense of smell in the recesses of our mind. Perhaps for this reason, the art of aromatherapy has re-emerged. It helps us seek balance by reacquainting us to the art of calm through scents, fragrances, aromas and smells that promote a profound sense of relaxation. Close your eyes and bring to mind the fragrance of lilac, mint or vanilla. A pleasing scent can take us away to another place, almost instantly.

Scientists acknowledge that the part of the brain that registers olfactory sensations borders a host of neurons that store memory. This is why when you catch the faintest whiff of tomato sauce cooking on the stove, you are immediately transported to your grandmother's kitchen. Or when you smell the aroma of the pipe tobacco in your father's study, all the warm comfortable feelings of your childhood memories are re-awakened.

Our ability to remember what we've smelled is stronger than our ability to recall what we've seen. Odors can improve recall by acting as retrieval cues. So when the brain encodes an event in memory, circumstances surrounding the event, such as images, sounds and odors are also encoded. Scientists believe that the brain's complex system for cataloging and identifying smells is closely linked to other areas involved in the storage of memories. Thus, smells, memories and emotions are certainly linked. Your sense of smell is astonishingly more acute than your sense of taste. Your nose can tell the difference among thousands of odors. Your tongue can only distinguish four tastes: salty, sour, bitter and sweet. You can even smell memories!

Although we may not think of using our sense of smell as a skill, like bowling, golf or word-processing, indeed, it is very much a skill used to promote relaxation. Have you ever watched a dog employ his sense of smell? Inside the house a dog may appear to be resting, but his sense of smell is on (most likely in search of food). Outside the house, dogs are all nose. When I walk my dog, I notice he doesn't just sniff, he sticks his nose in everything, being fully present with each scent. When relaxing through the sense of smell, we are invited to do the same.

Perhaps it's no coincidence that the sensation of smell is so closely tied to the breath, for it has long been known that breathing also promotes relaxation. Whether it's a deep sigh or a series of abdominal breaths, breathing combined with a pleasant smell is an unbeatable combination to practice the art of calm.

Not Just the Daily Grind

The alarm clock goes off. The news on the radio sounds like a re-broadcast of last year's headlines. Economic woes, social strife, environmental damage. It's Monday. The phone's ringing off the hook, and you haven't even made it to the office yet. Before the taste of coffee passes over your taste buds, the aroma of fresh ground coffee beans turns a potentially bad day into a mellow one. Whether you open a package yourself in the kitchen or you stop at the nearest coffee bar and pick up a cup, there is nothing like the smell of fresh ground coffee. Even those who are not coffee drinkers confide that they are often swayed in the direction of the aroma.

If the pace of work and career becomes a toxin to the spirit, then let the smell of fresh ground coffee be the antidote. Wake up and *really* smell the coffee. (Although coffee drinkers may spend hours debating the source of great coffee beans, the unofficial unanimous

vote goes to Kona coffee from the big island of Hawaii.) If you cannot grind your own beans, leave home a few minutes early, head to
the local coffee shop and just inhale.

A Call to the Sea

We spend nine months in a womb of salt water. We are made of the constituents found in every ocean. Perhaps for these reasons it is so relaxing to sit upon the shore of any beach and smell the cool salt air. For those who live by the sea, the nostrils may have acclimated, but whether you live close by the sea or make a pilgrimage to land's end, the refreshing wisp of salt air serves as a constant reminder that we are part of the whole—always connected. With that comes a sense of freedom, adventure and solitude.

If you have not made a pilgrimage to the sea in over a year, consider a trip east or west in your near future. When you find yourself standing on a dock, a pier or with your feet flirting with the sand and the foam, take a slow deep breath, letting the salt air fill your lungs with a sense of calm.

The Magic of Lavender

F lowers hold the essence of magic for the sense of smell. Although it may be hard to single out one flower's fragrance among the many with this gift, there are those who know that lavender is in a field by itself. Lavender holds the properties of calm and relaxation. In fact, it's often used in birthing rooms and maternity wards.

To the ancient mystics, lavender was known to promote relaxation and restore health. Today those who practice the art of aromatherapy will tell you the same thing. The French, who mastered the art of perfumes, knew the subtleties of essential oils and their capacity to evoke an emotional response. The beauty of essential oils is that they can be preserved, packaged and savored for use at any time.

When was the last time you smelled the fragrance of lavender? Find a store that carries lavender sachets and place one in your office desk or at home in a special place. When you get stressed, find some instant relief each time you open the drawer and take a deep breath.

Evergreens in Summer

Picture a cool summer morning in Maine. You find yourself walking along a shady path through a grove of white pines, balsams and spruce. The fog has lifted. The condensation of the morning dew accentuates the sweet scent of balsam fir, and as you take your next breath, you close your eyes to savor this sweet-scented aroma. For the next several moments this experience sends your spirits to new heights. You feel reborn.

Picture a warm summer afternoon in Colorado. You get out of your car to view the vista of rugged mountains clothed in blue spruce and green pine. Before you can fully adjust your eyes, you immediately detect the sweet scent of pine, and you close your eyes for a moment to enjoy.

Pine trees can be found in nearly every corner of the country. They are nature's gift of green during the winter months, and they bring the promise of abundance year round. Consider planting a new ever-green tree in your yard this year and harvest the sweet scent of pine, spruce or cedar as often as you can.

That Special Cookie,
Right from the Oven

Tollhouse, chocolate chip, peanut butter, almond or maca-roons. When heat is added to cookie dough for the right amount of time, magic occurs. The scent of fresh-baked cookies always seems directed to your nostrils, no matter how far away you are from the oven. Of course there are those memories of Mom's or Grandma's baked cookies—right after you built the winter's first snowman, or some slow weekend afternoon when only food will relieve the boredom of nothing good on television. Although some memories become embellished over time, there's nothing to exaggerate about how great home-baked cookies really smell.

So what are you waiting for? Preheat the oven. Pull out the flour, butter, eggs, sugar, walnuts and chocolate chips. Don't forget the coconut. Mix, stir and drop a big chunk of dough on the greased cookie sheet. Remember, make more than enough for everyone. Friends and neighbors show up like clockwork when the smell of fresh-baked cookies travels through the neighborhood. Don't forget the milk!

The Scent of Your Lover

SMELL · SMELL · SMELL · SMELL · SMELL · SMELL · SMELL · SMELL · SMELL · SMELL

Perhaps it's that special perfume you bought her last year for her birthday that drives you wild with passion. Perhaps it's the aftershave lotion he puts on every morning, or the cologne he wears on special occasions that makes you want to kiss and cuddle up. Maybe it's the lingering scent of detergent in her clothes that always makes you turn your head when the breeze catches it just right, or perhaps it's simply the fresh scent of salt and sweat beading up on his skin right after a workout. Perhaps it's the bath powder she uses, or the skin lotion she wears, or maybe it's the breath mint he chews before he kisses you.

The energy of love has many scents, each one accentuated with a touch of passion. Reawaken your sense of smell with the scent of your lover. To awaken his or her scent, try putting a little of your own on and see what happens.

96

Bathing by Candlelight

SMELL · SMELL · SMELL · SMELL · SMELL · SMELL · SMELL · SMELL · SMELL · SMELL

Vanilla. Pine. Rose. Orchid. Blueberry. Scented candles come in a host of fragrances. When the heat of the flame warms the wax of the candle, the fragrance used in the candle-making process is released to circulate freely in the air. The next time you are in the grocery store, stop in the aisle with the scented candles and pick up about ten. Then on a Tuesday evening set the candles carefully throughout the bathroom, light each one, draw the bath water to the right temperature, close the door, disrobe and step into the water, as your body is greeted by the splendid scent of candles. What a great midweek pick-me-up.

The Amber Nectar of Apples

Before one ever tastes the bittersweet nectar of cider, like a good wine, one must first smell the bouquet of ripe, aged-to-perfection apples. Perhaps there is no better way to serve cider than to add a touch of cinnamon, a smidgen of clove and just a hint of orange juice, all of which is then brought to a simmer over a hot stove. Sometimes all you need to do is keep a pot of cider warmed over a stove, allowing the scent to circulate throughout the house. During the fall and winter months when the Earth tilts its axis so that the days grow short, the smell of cider compensates for the lack of sunshine in the early twilight, and all is well.

From Texas with Love

Mesquite. This word brings a smile to the face of every Texan, every time. Mesquite, the only source of fuel for a real barbecue, comes from the mesquite tree, common to the Texas landscape. So popular is the aroma of its fibers when burned that it is a perennial favorite, not just in Texas, but wherever Texans have relocated, which is pretty darn near every state in the union. As if on a mission of goodwill, Texans have exported this resource so that all may enjoy its pleasures, from mesquite grills to mesquite briquettes.

Here is a suggestion, and you don't have to be from Texas to benefit. Find a store that sells mesquite briquettes and try a summer barbecue, or place a few mesquite wood chips in your fireplace this winter, then give a big Lone Star smile.

Spice Is Nice, and Then Some

SMELL · SMELL · SMELL · SMELL · SMELL · SMELL · SMELL · SMELL · SMELL · SMELL

I f variety is the spice of life, it can also be said that spice adds variety to life. Cloves. Allspice. Cilantro. Rosemary. Coriander. These are the makings of some fine aromas found in the kitchen (or from the backyard garden if you happen to grow them). Herbs, and the essential oils found in them, give off a potent scent. Because food is a pacifier and spices augment the taste of foods so greatly, it's a given that spices are a significant factor to promote relaxation.

Freshly picked spices tend to arouse the sense of smell because the essential oils are the most vibrant. Over time, the scent-carrying oils lose their punch (but not their taste).

Find a natural foods store where freshly dried herbs are sold. Take a few moments to smell the bouquet from each container. After surveying a broad sample, fill a small bag or two of spices that tickle your olfactory fancy. Then bring it home, place the open bag in the kitchen and let it do its magic. If so inspired, consider planting some herbs in your garden to bring some real spice into your life.

The Best Thing for a Cold

SMELL · SMELL · SMELL · SMELL · SMELL · SMELL · SMELL · SMELL · SMELL · SMELL

I t happens every year, sometimes more than once and always at the worst time. Stress is high, defenses are down, and *bam*, you get knocked off your feet with a cold, or worse, the flu. Homemade chicken soup (also known as Jewish penicillin), an old folk remedy, may be nothing more than a placebo, but anyone who has had a cold knows just how good a cup of this low-tech medicine really is. Is it the protein molecules from the chicken meat that help produce more white blood cells, or is it some special pheromone riding on a wave of chicken broth that begins to activate the immune system well before the soup is ingested? We may never really know. To be honest, it doesn't matter. Most likely it is the synergy of all active ingredients that combine forces for a healing effect. But this we do know: home-made chicken soup smells great no matter what shape your immune system is in, particularly on the cold gray days of winter.

Magic Carpet Ride

SMELL · SMELL · SMELL · SMELL · SMELL · SMELL · SMELL · SMELL · SMELL · SMELL

From the dawn of humanity, incense has been considered a sacred medium to heighten the sense of smell and lower the threshold of excitement to a comfortable sense of calm. A gift from monarchs and travelers alike, today incense can be found in all corners of the world. From the altars of temples and chapels to private rooms where one sits and meditates, the smell of burning incense brings with it a familiarity of comfort and relaxation. Although some scents are rather strong, the calming power of incense is its subtle aroma as a tiny column of smoke wafts toward the ceiling. Some people add burning incense to their ritual of meditation. Others simply use it as a form of air-freshener.

Sandalwood, vanilla and jasmine are three of the many popular scents. If you are looking for that special something to serve as a reminder to calm down, open a window, light a stick of incense and let your spirit take a magic carpet ride to tranquility.

Did Someone Say "Barbecue"?

It's summertime or darn close to it. The afternoon thunderstorm has just cleared. The air is fresh and appetites peak. There really is no choice about what to make for dinner. It's time for a barbecue! What is so tempting about a barbecue? Most people will tell you it's the sauce: a magical blend of tomatoes, spices and ingredients known only to a chosen few. There are contests around the country to determine who makes the best barbecue sauce. Winners and runners-up are not prone to share their secret ingredients. But rest assured, whatever it is, the end result reaches the nose before the mouth can even begin to salivate.

Barbecues are great any time of year, no matter what kind of sauce you use. So what are you waiting for?

Campfires and Memories

I'm convinced that a gene in our DNA activates the relaxation response while we sit near a campfire late at night. Scientists are on the verge of announcing their findings any day. The smell of burning logs, whether they are pine, oak, maple, birch or aspen, activates this gene, particularly on cool summer and fall evenings when the stars are bright. The smoke rises toward the heavens, but not before it fills your nostrils and permeates your clothes.

Reach back into your memory bank and you may recall that as a young child your first exposure to a campfire was enchanting. And long after the flames were put out, the smell of burning logs stayed with you, on your hands, your hair and most definitely your clothes. Take a deep breath and remind yourself of that smell, then close your eyes and let your mind drift away to a quiet place beside a campfire.

Hot Chocolate on a Cold Day

If there is a gift to the olfactory senses, surely chocolate is one such gift. Although this divine pleasure captivates the senses in many forms, from cake icings to candies and ice cream, the aroma of real hot chocolate, mixed with milk, on a cold day is unbeatable. Perhaps it brings back fond early childhood memories. Perhaps it reminds you of a sense of comfort. Regardless of the reason, the smell of hot chocolate on a cold day is a great temporary panacea for most any troubles.

Has the maddening pace of life got you down in the holiday season? Stop what you're doing and direct your feet toward a coffee or sandwich shop and ask for a cup of hot chocolate (with whipped cream and cinnamon). Of course the best option is to fix a cup when you get home. Either way, take your time with it. Smell the aroma before each sip. Smile as you realize you have just regained your sense of composure.

A Rose by Any Other Name . . .

S hakespeare had it right. A rose by any other name would surely smell as sweet. So heavenly is the scent of the rose that it is coveted as the greatest of all flowers. You don't have to be in love to enjoy roses either. We may think of roses on Valentine's Day, but the scent of the rose is equally nice in bath oils, soaps, potpourri, massage oil and sachets. The fragrance of roses is a must for everyone, anytime. No thorny issue, the symbol of the rose is unconditional love, the highest love of all. So do yourself a favor today, buy yourself a rose (or rose product) and wear the scent proudly. You are beautiful!

Blue Skies and Autumn Decadence

SMELL · SMELL · SMELL · SMELL · SMELL · SMELL · SMELL · SMELL · SMELL · SMELL

Remember when you jumped into your first pile of raked leaves? Ascending into the last breath of a vibrant maple or ash? Leaves decay into soil creating an unmistakable smell. Like most smells that take us back to a time of comfort, the crisp pitch of autumn leaves is a one-way ticket to childhood, a time embedded with wonder and awe, or beauty and mystery, and a blue sky without end. As we mature into adulthood and take with us all the baggage of responsibility, we tend to lose the spontaneity and wonder of life. But this is nothing that a quick jump into a pile of autumn leaves cannot cure. If a pile of leaves is not readily accessible, walk into a floral shop and search with your nose for a similar smell. Don't worry, you'll find it.

What Rhymes with Orange?

Folklore reminds us that when the rays of sunlight first kissed the buds of the orange blossom, the tree wept in joy. The tradition continues to this very day. Oranges are the collection of these teardrops. Orange juice is said to be the nectar of the gods. And the fragrance of the orange blossom can literally lift you off your feet.

Can you smell sunshine? Sure! Through the gift of orange teardrops. The next time you're in the grocery store, pick up several oranges. When you get home, cut or peel the skin off one, pause for a moment, inhale and smell the rind. Then smile. The orange must be a special fruit, for no word rhymes with it. Certainly, nothing compares.

A Harvest Moon and October Delights

Pumpkins are usually spherical in shape—the universal symbol of wholeness. Getting a pumpkin to reveal its festive Halloween face requires getting your hands intimate with the fruit of the pumpkin, squeezing its pulp, sifting its seeds and inhaling the aroma of fresh pumpkin meat. If the last time you smelled the inside of a pumpkin was in your childhood, there is definitely some catching up to do. If you missed even one cycle in the rotation of the harvest moon (another symbol of wholeness), it's time to step into the rhythm of the season.

Go out and buy a pumpkin this autumn (preferably at a pumpkin patch but any grocery store will have them). Select one big enough to stick your hand in, then pull out a knife and cut open the top. The harvest moon awaits you inside.

Deep Forest, Light Rain

On a late spring or early summer day, when the skies turn gray and the clouds have already begun to cry, grab a friend, hop in your car and drive to the nearest state park or forest. Agree to roam together, but take a vow of silence until you come back to the car. Walk casually to the edge of the forest and step in. Smell the forest come alive with a thousand different scents and fragrances. Count in your mind how many you can detect or observe. Is it the leaves, the bark, the pine needles? Is it the moist earth, the berries or the dew itself? What do you smell? With each step into the forest, leave behind an issue, problem or concern that has hijacked your attention for the past several hours and instead find your balance in nature.

Koalas Have a Clue

Once, on a trip to Australia, I had the opportunity to hold a koala in my arms. Although at first I was charmed with this small but heavy, mellow creature, within seconds I was intoxicated with the scent of the eucalyptus leaves he was chewing. "Billy" the koala was high on the juice of the gum tree.

You don't have to travel anywhere or cuddle a koala to know the subtle beauty of eucalyptus leaves. Their fragrance is quite unmistakable. Eucalyptus leaves do more than just clear your sinuses, they cleanse the air, which is why many people place dried arrangements in their homes and offices. Floral shops carry them, as do some hobby shops. So if you're looking for a nice change, try the gift from Down Under and place them in containers around your house. G'day mate!

Wednesday Is Spaghetti Day

Decades ago a popular marketing slogan read, "Wednesday is Prince Spaghetti Day." It wasn't long before I noticed that all around the neighborhood, Italian or not, everybody ate spaghetti on Wednesdays. If there was a smell associated with a particular day of the week, it would be spaghetti sauce on Wednesdays. It was great to walk into my friends' homes and smell tomatoes simmering on the stove. Oregano, basil and parsley ready to be tossed in. Let's not forget a generous helping of fresh garlic.

In the fast-paced lives we live, it may seem easier to just open a can or bottle of pre-made sauce, but following a recipe for spaghetti sauce is really a stress-management program in disguise. It begins with mental imagery (imagine how good it smells and tastes) and ends with a heartwarming meal that appeases the appetite. Mark your calendar for next Wednesday and every Wednesday thereafter.

Freshly Mowed Grass

SMELL · SMELL · SMELL · SMELL · SMELL · SMELL · SMELL · SMELL · SMELL · SMELL

Grass: a carpet of lush green vegetation, a sea of tranquility surrounding houses, trailers and castles alike. Grass is the homeowner's common denominator. Perhaps nothing sends the mind daydreaming more quickly than gazing at a yard or field of emerald green grass. And what it is that sends the mind to seventh heaven upon smelling freshly cut grass remains a mystery, but rest assured, this aroma is one of nature's most pleasurable scents.

Some say that it's the scent in the moisture that the grass releases when trimmed. Others say it is reminiscent of early childhood memories where outdoor play was first introduced. Still others cite the dynamics of photosynthesis. The mystery needn't be solved, only enjoyed when possible. So take a walk in your neighborhood tonight and see if your nose leads you to a street corner where the grass has been neatly trimmed and memories call you back to your childhood.

Spanking New!

What is so irresistible about the smell of a newborn baby, especially after a bath? Strangers and friends alike will approach a newborn hoping to catch the scent of newness. What looks like a chance to get a closer look is really an attempt to catch that essence of freshness once more.

By our very nature, we have an affinity for the smell of newness (as well as the old). Topping the list: the smell of new clothes, new cars, new homes, a new office, new puppies and kittens and, of course, at the top of the list, new babies. Try to find something new today. Inhale as many times as you like. Ask yourself, what is it that attracts you to this? Perhaps it's the newness that is a symbolic reminder to clean our emotional slate and start anew as well. If, in your search today, you happen to find a new baby to enjoy, consider yourself one lucky person.

Sunshine and Palm Trees

More people spend vacations by the beach than at any other location. It's the water, the sunshine and perhaps; most of all, the freedom to come and go as you please. Aside from the salt air, is there a smell associated with the beach? The answer is yes; it's suntan lotion, specifically coconut oil. One whiff of coconut oil and you are under the spell of the sun god, not to mention the salt air, the sand and the foam. Coconut oil is the smell of carefree summer days.

Coconut oil may not be a conventional scent for aromatherapy, but it works wonders, whether you're lying on the beach or need a quick respite during a twelve-hour workday. If you are landlocked for the next few months with no beach in sight, then try traveling by means of the sense of smell to the shores where you'll find plenty of sunshine, palm trees and coconut oil.

The First Hint of Snow

You smell it before you ever see it. In Colorado, it happens in late October; on rare exceptions, late September. The sun sinks a little farther south each day. The clouds, when they appear, become more ominous. You could be outside for a jog, or perhaps just retrieving the mail or getting into your car to drive home from work. As you turn your head, you catch a subtle change in the air, not temperature, not moisture. A freshness. Snow!

The first hint of snow arrives on a breath of fresh air. It signals clarity, symbolizes cleansing and promises newness. One breath of premonition does all that, for some at least.

The first snow brings with it many perceptions, but the most relaxing is that of a clean slate and a feeling of tranquility. Can you smell snow in the air? You won't know until you head outdoors. When you do, take the hint.

FOUR

Relaxing Through the Sense of Taste

Swiss chocolate. Ripe strawberries. Mountain stream water. Both food and drink serve to pacify the stress response, transforming a cry to a sigh and an "Oh my God!" to "Oh God, this is so good." In today's rushed lifestyle, people rarely take the time to actually taste the food passing over the tongue. Rather, today's eating habits can best be described as either "inhaling" or "wolfing" processed to-go foods. Savoring the rich taste, texture and temperature of culinary morsels is a diminishing art, as is culinary artistry itself (on average two of the three meals eaten today are prepared outside the home).

So how does food instill a sense of relaxation? Simple. By combining foods and beverages that titillate the taste buds and give pause for thought. With the conscious choice to allow these morsels and fluids to gently pass over the lips and tongue, the stress response is quickly deactivated.

The art of calm with this sense begins by locating stores and food outlets that carry those items that, quite literally, deliver the goods. Make a habit of exploring new markets which stock a variety of tantalizing goodies. Rather than become a creature of habit in which you tend to eat the same foods each day, get out and explore new stores, specialty markets and start gazing through cookbooks.

Each of the 7,000 taste buds on your tongue is waiting for a new experience. Tap into your "hunter and gatherer" energies to explore new horizons for your taste buds. Not only will your mouth thank you, but your mind, body and spirit will as well.

Just Desserts

Crème brûleé, chocolate mousse, tiramisu, lemon meringue pie, cannoli, blueberry crepes à la mode. Is your mouth watering yet? I read somewhere that there are more taste buds with a sensitivity for sweets than for any other taste. If it's true, then common sense would dictate there must be a reason for this. I know many people would say that sweets are essential for emotional well-being. I can vouch for this. Take chocolate, for example.

Other than taste, timing is important, too, otherwise desserts would be the main entree and salads and such would follow. But we know this isn't true. The order of a meal is analogous to the order of life. We tend to avoid things we don't like and save many of the best things to the very end. After all, if it weren't the case, we'd have nothing to look forward to. There is an important lesson in desserts, a lesson in delayed gratification. Patience is a virtue. Food is a metaphor for life. Sometimes the best things are worth waiting for.

A Hint of Mint

For millennia, long before the advent of toothpaste, mint was an herb used to cleanse the palate and freshen the breath. Its taste was quite powerful. To chew on a mint leaf for a few moments seemed not only to clean the mouth, but to clear the mind as well. It almost had a euphoric flavor. Today, so common is its use that mint can be found in chewing gum, breath mints, toothpaste, mouthwashes, toothpicks and even some herbal teas.

But have you ever tried the real thing? The taste of fresh mint leaves is truly refreshing. A little bit goes a long way. Explore a neighborhood herb or spice garden some Sunday afternoon and stroll through the rows of plants. Let your eyes guide your taste buds (you might even consider growing some in your own garden). Tear a small section of a mint leaf and place it on your tongue. Begin chewing the leaf to release the juice from the fiber of the plant. Close your eyes and focus your complete attention on the taste of mint. Then say "ahh!" You will be pleasantly surprised.

A Downeast Tradition

I am not a native Mainer, I'm from "away." But while I attended college there, I acquired a taste for the one export that has made the state famous: lobster (or as they say Downeast, lohbstaahh).

One thing I did learn about lobster is the correct way to eat it—and it's not in a fancy restaurant. A Downeast lobster (trapped fresh that day) is eaten outside on a picnic table, preferably by the ocean, with a loaf of bread and an ear of corn. Nothing fancy, because you're supposed to place your full attention on the taste of the sea: one of salt, minerals and romance. The brown crustacean boiled to a deep red, when pulled out of its shell (and dipped in melted butter), simply dissolves in your mouth. There really is no better way. This alone is worth a trip to Maine. However, if the northern tip of New England is not on your travel itinerary anytime soon, don't let this stop you from re-creating the scene at home. The bib is optional!

Fresh Strawberries Dipped in Chocolate

TASTE · TASTE · TASTE · TASTE · TASTE · TASTE · TASTE · TASTE · TASTE · TASTE · TASTE

When it comes to food, if you're going to sin, go all the way. You cannot get much more decadent than fresh strawberries dipped in rich, dark chocolate. The temptation is worth the caloric risk. Besides, this extravagance requires no repentance, only joy! When did these two unlikely items get paired up in a culinary pas de deux?

If history serves us correctly, a chef on the French-Swiss border was experimenting with the combinations of several tastes when he came upon a winner. The result: the mildly sweet taste of the fresh strawberry combined with the bittersweet taste of Swiss chocolate. And the rest is history.

Unless you fix these yourself (and it's not that hard to do—just keep the strawberries chilled before dipping and select really fine chocolate), you're most likely to find this delicacy at state dinners or black-tie events, often served with coffee, just before dessert. After all, fresh strawberries dipped in chocolate are the taste of pure elegance. Why not dress for the occasion?

Succulent Fruits

TASTE · TASTE · TASTE · TASTE · TASTE · TASTE · TASTE · TASTE · TASTE · TASTE · TASTE

Fruits are summer's gifts for a warm mouth in search of relief. Oranges, grapefruits, grapes, pineapple, honeydew, cantaloupe and watermelon, along with a host of other fruits hold an oasis of taste in their juices. Combine that with the lush meat of the fruit and you're one bite closer to heaven. In the economy of taste, you get more bang for your buck or, more simply, more tang for your tongue. The fructose, vitamins and minerals are an added bonus.

So what do you get when you mix these fruits together? A masterpiece. An outstanding fruit salad. Don't let the prep work of cutting pieces of pineapple or curling balls of cantaloupe stop you before you start. With your knife as a paintbrush, think of yourself as an artist creating a masterpiece—still-life salad with succulent fruits. Your palette might include the mellow orange meat of cantaloupe, the sweet red sugar of watermelon, the lush green nectar of honeydew and grapes and the honeyed yellow juice of pineapple. By now your mouth should be watering. Likes attract. So what are you waiting for?

Happy as a Clam (at High Tide)

New England fishermen have always known what to eat after an exhausting day on the high seas. Especially on a cold winter's night, as temperatures plummet and appetites soar, clam chowder becomes a calming meal in itself. (Is it coincidence that *clam* and *calm* are nearly the same word?)

Sorry Campbell's, but authentic New England clam chowder cannot be equaled. It's a hearty blend of salty, creamy goodness. Complimentary warm flavors that balance the mind, body and spirit. You can find a simple recipe in most cookbooks, but the secret to the best clam chowder is the consistency of the soup—not too watery, not too creamy. Of course, chunks of potatoes add stick-to-your-bones body. Let's not forget the clams. Melted butter, oregano, a pinch of salt, parsley and coarsely ground pepper for good measure. Stew lovingly over a hot stove. Soup's on!

Hunting and Gathering

TASTE · TASTE · TASTE · TASTE · TASTE · TASTE · TASTE · TASTE · TASTE · TASTE · TASTE

Where I grew up, my sisters and I would spend a lazy weekend afternoon foraging the forest in search of wild berries. Oh, the joy to come across a blueberry patch, a wild raspberry patch or, on a rare occasion, wild strawberries. The search for the perfect berry was akin to the search for the Holy Grail. If truth be told, the best berries never made it back home to be made into jelly.

Eating a berry is like smelling a flower. To enjoy it fully, it must be eaten individually, so as to appreciate the synergy of sweetness, succulent juice and, of course, the texture each berry brings to the mouth. Wrap your mouth around one tiny wild berry, compress the juice with your tongue against the roof of your mouth. It's nothing less than sensuous.

Although roadside berry patches are on the endangered species list, if you look hard enough, you can find a place where you can pick your own berries in spring, summer or fall. Of course it's all the better when you find them in the wild. So grab a basket and head into the woods.

That's-a-Nice!

sk any child his or her favorite food, and you're likely to hear the word *spaghetti*. They don't just say it. They yell it: SPAGHETTI!

Adults typically feel the same way about spaghetti with sauce yet they are just more reserved with their feelings. What is the attraction to pasta? Is it the sauce? No! Is it the meatball? Maybe. Is it the noodles as they slip between the lips, past the tongue and glide down the throat? You got it. Pasta, pasta, pasta! A magical blend of creamy tomato sauce lubricates each noodle, allowing for the primo "slurp effect," paisano. Never mind the specks of red spaghetti sauce flicked on shirts and ties. Kids don't think of these things. Perhaps adults shouldn't either. A little violin serenade, candlelight and "bellisimo."

The Earl of Grey

Many foods grab the attention of our taste buds and leave us wanting more. Other tastes, however, are more subtle, yet equally dynamic in stature. Such is the nature of teas, specifically the tea Earl Grey, named after a royal figure centuries ago who understood the power of subtle tastes. With just the right mixture of oil of bergamot, Earl had a hit on his hands. A tea was named after him and the rest is history.

There is an art to fine tea drinking. First, the preferred brand is always nice (my favorite is Celestial Seasonings, however, my friends vote for Stash). Next is flavor. I prefer Earl Grey, but chamomile is also very calming. Remember, for tea to reach its greatest potential, it must be brewed with piping hot water and steeped for no less than five minutes, longer if possible. The heat allows the essential oils to be released from the tea leaves. It is the oil which, in its own subtle way, calls to the taste buds to relax. The whole body follows.

Equally important is the way you drink your tea. Take a brief pause from your daily grind at mid-morning (10:00 A.M.) and again at 4:00 P.M. (known throughout the world as high tea). Sit in a big, comfortable chair and serve yourself delectable desserts and delicate finger sandwiches. Follow the lead of the folks in the countries of the former British empire where everything ceases for tea time. Try a cup today and give a nod to the Earl of teas.

Ice Cream Therapy

TASTE · TASTE · TASTE · TASTE · TASTE · TASTE · TASTE · TASTE · TASTE · TASTE · TASTE

You've heard of retail therapy, where shopping relieves the temporary stress of life. You've heard of hydrotherapy, where submersion into a tub of hot water soothes the body. But have you heard of ice cream therapy?

Scientists have now discovered a direct link between the tongue and the hypothalamus (the seat of the emotions), and in clinically controlled laboratory tests (double-blind studies, no less), ten out of ten subjects reported feeling better after eating ice cream. Control subjects given ricotta cheese reported no change in emotion. The results were conclusive (smile). Ice cream therapy works.

Scientists isolated several factors in the ice cream proven to be responsible for altered mood, including the quality of cream used, the flavor added to the cream, the texture of the cream-to-tongue ratio, the sugar quotient and last, but not least, the brand name (Ben & Jerry's won top honors). Pick up a pint today.

This Pizza Is Not Delivered to Just Anyone

I'm talking about the best pizza, the kind made with love. Real finger food. The kind where you need fifteen napkins to make it through a meal. I'm talking about chewy dough, not dry. And sauce, plenty of it, that thick, slow, juicy paste that doesn't run. The cheese (pay attention because this is important) has to be gooey and stretch from your mouth to your hand, no matter how long your arm is. As far as toppings go, this is surely a matter of personal choice, but may I put a vote in for pineapple and ham. I know it sounds strange, but trust me on this. It works. Especially if someone else makes the pizza.

Perhaps it's the flood of childhood memories that brings a smile to your face with each bite. Maybe it's the alchemy of cheese, tomato, wheat, special toppings and the idea that the weekend is here. Or perchance it's the romantic Italian spirit unleashed when you open the box or oven door. All this and more awaits you with the next slice.

The Best Popcorn

TASTE • TASTE • TASTE • TASTE • TASTE • TASTE • TASTE • TASTE • TASTE • TASTE • TASTE

Contrary to popular belief, movie theaters do not have the best popcorn. The best popcorn requires butter, not some synthetic oil substitute. While you wait for the late movie on TV some evening, open the fridge and pull out the butter. Set one burner to simmer for the butter, the other on high for the golden kernels (or do the easy microwave technique). In moments you have harvested a midnight feast. Add a touch of salt and you're set. The first kernel of popped corn, dripping in melted butter, lands in your mouth and you are in heaven.

So the next late night when you've got the hungries, and so do your kids (who by all rights should be asleep by now, but it's Friday night and the rules are bent), and your stomach is rumbling for a few more morsels of food before the system shuts down for the night, think popcorn—the best popcorn.

Start Spreading the Word

TASTE · TASTE · TASTE · TASTE · TASTE · TASTE · TASTE · TASTE · TASTE · TASTE · TASTE

Cheese is an acquired taste. As a rule, infants do not gravitate toward anything fermented. On the other hand, children do have an attraction for all things sweet. So who ever thought you could put cheese into a dessert?

While growing up, I refused even a bite of New York-style cheese-cake. I thought it was a conspiracy to get children to eat things they really didn't like. I knew that if I were to succumb to cheesecake, then asparagus cake wasn't far behind. And God forbid the day my parents brought out Brussels sprouts cake. I even began disliking the state of New York for taking part in this conspiracy.

So you can imagine my surprise when as a college student I reluctantly had my first bite of this enchanted dessert. I discovered the ingredients included a mystical blend of cream cheese, sugar (and honey), eggs, vanilla extract, fresh ginger and heavy cream. Oh my

God, was this good! The first taste was exhilarating. By the second bite, I was seduced. By the third, a convert. I even planned a trip to the Big Apple to get the real thing. New York, New York. The city so great they named it twice. My favorite kind of cheesecake, you ask? Well, New York-style cheesecake with fresh blueberries and a dollop of homemade whipped cream. Need I say more? Quick, call me a taxi.

In Honor of Turkey and Mashed Potatoes

Now maybe it's simply the idea of eating great food all day long that decreases your sympathetic neural drive on Thanksgiving Day. Or perhaps it's the tryptophan in the meal itself that surrenders you to a comatose state by day's end, but it's not inaccurate to say that there is a predetermined relaxation quotient on Turkey Day before you ever start eating a morsel of gratitude.

The tongue likes texture as well as flavor, which is why Thanksgiving is such a celebration for the mouth. It is said in the East that when two opposites come together, they don't fight in opposition, rather they form a union or whole. And *what* a union with mashed potatoes (soft and creamy) and turkey (dense and chewy).

Turkey without mashed potatoes is a travesty to the tongue! Make a wish right now to eat the next turkey meal with a mound of mashed potatoes (and gravy) and taste the opposites as they attract. You don't have to wait until November either.

Nothing to Wine About

Take thousands of Sangiovese grapes growing in a valley in the Tuscany region of Italy. Harvest them, press them and age the juice well for a few years. Keep it in a tinted bottle away from sunlight.

The coveted bottle of red wine arrives on your dining table. Perhaps it's a gift from someone who will share its magic. The food is served. The evening meal is underway and the wine is poured gently into each goblet. You raise your glass, make a toast and bring the wine to your lips. The taste is pleasantly sweet, but not overwhelming. Close your eyes for a moment and sigh. This is how wine is supposed to taste. Make a toast to life.

Et Tu Fait?

Pardonez moi, my French leaves a little bit to be desired. And you? When asked what foods provided a sense of calm, several of my students (most likely the ones from New Orleans or those who went to Mardi Gras) listed *etouffée*. Never having been to the Big Easy, I had to inquire, "Qu'est que c'est?" They were astonished! "Mon Dieu!" Shame on me. As of now, I am more cultured.

Now correct me if I'm wrong, but don't spicy foods make you perspire? Sweating is part of the stress response, not the relaxation response. My students were unyielding. "You've got to try it," they insisted. So for those of you who like to stress your taste buds so they can then relax, this recipe for etouffée is for you. I'm going to let you judge this one for yourself. Bon appétit!

144

1 stick of butter

1 lb. peeled crawfish or shrimp

Tony's Creole seasoning, add
  liberally

1 tablespoon paprika

1 medium onion, chopped

1 green pepper, chopped

2 cloves garlic, minced

2 cups water

1 tablespoon finely chopped
  onion tops

1 tablespoon finely chopped
  parsley

Melt butter in a deep, thick aluminum frying pan. Season crawfish or shrimp with seasoning and paprika. Add to butter and cook two to three minutes. Remove crawfish/shrimp and set aside. Next, add chopped onion, pepper and garlic to pot. Sauté well for at least ten minutes. Return crawfish or shrimp to pot and add two cups of water. Stir and cook slowly for about forty minutes (add more water if needed). Serve on boiled rice and sprinkle with minced onion tops and parsley. Serves four, or two hungry jazz musicians.

A Cold Drink on a Hot Day

TASTE · TASTE · TASTE · TASTE · TASTE · TASTE · TASTE · TASTE · TASTE · TASTE · TASTE

High temperatures (not to mention humidity) can bring stress to the body, giving new meaning to the expression, "the day from hell"—the exact opposite of calm. Heat stress combined with all the other kinds of stress you face each day can be oppressive. But it doesn't have to be!

One of the best ways to cool down is with a tall iced glass of freshly squeezed lemonade. Don't forget to add just enough sugar to balance the bitterness of the lemons. Not only does this recipe for stress quench your thirst by lowering your core body temperature, but making lemonade with fresh lemons sends an unconscious message to change perceptions about other stressors, too.

For an extra twist, try mixing half a glass of lemonade with half a glass of iced tea. If making fresh lemonade seems like too much work, fear not! Bottled lemonade does the trick just as well.

My Kingdom for an Egg

There is a legend from a faraway land that tells us a story about the chicken and the egg (with no resolution on which came first, I might add). It appears that one day the gods gave us chickens so we could share in the bounty of their eggs. Eggs are esteemed as one of the perfect nutrients, despite the cholesterol. All that aside, eggs are a real treat for the sense of taste. When you think of all the possibilities of cooking eggs, the list seems almost endless: fried, scrambled, poached, hard-boiled, soft-boiled, quiched, Benedicted, huevose'd and for those daring, raw (organic only please). An egg, an egg, my kingdom for an egg. Quick, ask one of the neighbors.

How would you go about describing the taste of eggs? It's not easy. A mild gushy pleasant taste? Neither sweet nor salty. Firm, yet pliable. Smooth on the tongue and easy on the teeth. The taste of a new day full of possibilities, eggs are, indeed, one of the treasures of the food world.

147

Fresh Bread from the Oven

TASTE · TASTE · TASTE · TASTE · TASTE · TASTE · TASTE · TASTE · TASTE · TASTE · TASTE

I t is said that we cannot live by bread alone but, hey, it's a good start. There's a small bakery tucked in a corner of Boulder, Colorado, that sells the best fresh-baked bread west of the Mississippi. People drive for miles to stand in line at the crack of dawn. I know because I am there, too! As one fellow customer once said, "To taste that warm bread with fresh melted butter is to know nirvana."

Make it a point to find a neighborhood bakery this week that sells fresh bread. Find out when the loaves come out of the oven, budget your time accordingly, perhaps even arrive a few minutes early. Bring your own butter if you want. Break off a chunk and plan to become transformed.

Come Home to Vermont

Autumn in Vermont. Maples and birches ablaze in color everywhere. Then the first winter winds send the leaves dancing to earth. In winter, the Green Mountains turn white in a deep blanket of bright snow.

Long after the trees drop their leaves, the sap from the maple trees pools in the trunk, sitting, waiting for spring. Native Americans first discovered the secret that the bare sugar maples held. By boiling the sap, they turned the pale liquid into gold. Today, anything less than pure maple syrup on pancakes, waffles, crêpes or French toast is a crime.

Real maple syrup is as close as your nearest grocery store. Yes, it costs more, but it's worth it. Now on Sunday morning, when you pull out the eggs and pancake mix, reach for the real maple syrup. Remember, Vermonters heat their syrup; it brings out the flavor even more.

Licorice, the Real Thing

TASTE · TASTE · TASTE · TASTE · TASTE · TASTE · TASTE · TASTE · TASTE · TASTE · TASTE

Some tastes are simply indescribable. Licorice is one of them. Dime-store candies imitate the flavor of licorice but, in truth, licorice is one of the most popular and widely consumed herbs in the world. Licorice grows wild in southern and central Europe and Asia. It's widely known for its ability to calm an upset stomach. But most people don't know it can also be used to relieve upper respiratory infections and symptoms of menopause.

Licorice is a perennial. Its white to blue-violet flowers and the roots yield the licorice. Most likely you can buy dried licorice in a health food store and munch on it. You can also find the taste of licorice in some herbal teas. Like mint, licorice tends to bring a sense of freshness to your mouth. And on a particularly hot day, when your sluggish appetite needs a jump-start, try savoring the real thing.

Don't Eat the Yellow Snow

Italian ice. You've heard about it, but have you ever tried it? Now's your chance. The best time to indulge in this heavenly creation is on a hot day, when your thirst requests a hint of sweetness. Orange, raspberry, pineapple, lime, passion fruit—what's your pleasure?

Here's the technique: You hold a freshly scooped ice delight and anticipate. First your tongue hits the cone of delicately shaved ice and you smile. As your tongue pulls in a few shavings of ice, the water melts in your mouth and cascades down your throat. The taste buds have reached nirvana; the rest of your mouth isn't far behind. If it turns out there is no Italian ice stand nearby, the next best thing is a fruit smoothie (Jamaican ice). Ask for extra ice.

Who Made the Salad?

Cucumbers, carrots, celery, cabbage, red peppers, lettuce, spinach, onions—these foods speak of texture. Although veggies themselves may not exactly do a tap dance on the head of your taste buds, their contribution to taste in terms of texture is subtle, yet very important. Besides there is always salad dressing. Texture is to the tongue what color is to the eyes, and veggies have texture galore: carrots are crunchy; celery is fibrous; cucumbers are tough on the outside but soft on the inside; radishes are dense; peppers snap in your mouth. Mixed together, the combination of textures is a jubilee for the mouth.

Beyond the tongue and mouth, vegetables become even more important as they work their way down the esophagus and gastrointestinal tract. Remember, fiber is your friend. So it's agreed upon, the goal is to eat more veggies, organic if you can.

The Best Thirst Quencher

Water. Fresh cool water. Your mouth salivates at the thought of it. Above all other beverages, water is the number one thirst quencher. Although it can be argued that water really has no taste, the truth is, it does. The optimal taste is wet cool freshness—a subjective quality that is hard, by any standards, to argue with.

Sad to say the quality of water on our planet has diminished greatly over the years. Tap water today often tastes as if it comes from a swimming pool rather than from a clear mountain stream. Bottled water may be no better.

If you long for the wet, cool taste of fresh mountain water, the kind that Lewis and Clark tasted on their trek across the continent centuries ago, a good water filtration system in your kitchen is worth considering. Drink up.

The Tree of Life

To participate in the harvest is to complete the circle. Come early fall, if you live where apples ripen on the trees, invite some friends and find a friendly orchard. Unlike produce in the grocery store, when you pluck an apple from a tree, you know immediately where the fruit came from. To really enjoy the once-forbidden fruit is a true meditative experience. First, the sight of the perfect apple, then the feel of this special fruit, followed by the sweet smell. Reach up. Snap it off. Then move your hand to your face, open your mouth and sink your teeth in. Time stands still. Ripe autumn apples are magical.

Did I Mention Chocolate Yet?

Chocolate is the food of the gods. It's true, chocolate arouses all the senses. Research at Harvard indicates that chocolate contains antioxidants and promotes longevity. Rumor has it that the vibration of chocolate even clears all the chakras and meridians as well. My, this is divine!

Chocolate is sweet, creamy, chewy and melts in your mouth. And oh, the memories and emotions it evokes, like love, happiness, bliss, ecstasy—chocolate is heaven on earth. There are so many active ingredients in chocolate, it would take volumes to explain why the taste is indescribable. But who needs theory? I myself prefer experiential knowledge. To be honest I don't know if my data collection will ever be complete. Mocha, amaretto, Swiss, German, Belgian, Godiva, Rocky Mountain, Champlain. May the search never end!

FIVE

Relaxing Through the Sense of Touch

The sense of touch is so important that infants would die without it. By our very nature, the sense of touch is essential for life, not only through our fingers, but every square inch of our bodies.

As we move deeper into the age of high technology, the sense of touch will play a greater role, some say, in maintaining levels of optimal health. Keyboards and number pads alone won't cut it. Perhaps for this reason, there is a rapidly growing interest in the area of body-work, particularly massage therapy. With muscle tension being the number one symptom of stress, massage therapy is the first line of defense to counteract the ills of the computer desk jockey or any other job where enforced stillness of the body produces tension.

Although a massage is nothing less than heavenly, massage therapy is only the beginning of using the sense of touch to enter a state of calm. Taking a hot bath, soaking in a Jacuzzi, or lying on a feather bed can be equally relaxing. Let's not forget a comforting hug in times of need. And then again for some, all it takes is holding the TV remote in one's hand to reach a state of bliss.

In terms of surface area, the skin is our largest organ. Moreover, muscles also make up a fair amount of tissue that rely on touch. When the needs of these two organs are combined, the importance of the sense of touch becomes quite obvious. Temperature and humidity play a tremendous role in comfort levels as well.

The role of touch and its importance as the essential quotient of calm cannot be understated.

Pet Therapy

Eric was a star football player in high school until a tackle brought him down, snapping his neck and leaving him a quadriplegic. The first night I met Eric, he rolled into my class and right alongside him was his dog, Major. We struck up a conversation about dogs, for I had just adopted Shasta, a four-year-old husky who joined me in class that same night. As Shasta and Major sniffed and greeted, Eric shared with me his reason for getting a pet. Primarily it was for the company, but it also gave him the opportunity to enjoy the touch of a thick coat of fur.

"My hands have little sensitivity, but from my neck up, it's heaven," he said with a smile.

People tend to gravitate to animals, and whether it's a cat, dog, bird or horse, the desire to touch and make physical contact is healing. People who own pets are known to be healthier. Eric testifies to the fact that pets promote relaxation. He says he's more mellow now with Major by his side. Eric knows how to share a good thing. He often makes trips to nursing homes so Major can make the rounds. Pet therapy: don't leave home without it. If you don't own a pet but want a pet therapy session, try visiting a pet store, volunteering at an animal shelter or stopping by to see a friend who owns a cat or dog.

Shaking Hands, Holding Hands

TOUCH · TOUCH · TOUCH · TOUCH · TOUCH · TOUCH · TOUCH · TOUCH · TOUCH · TOUCH

The palm is the heart of the hand. When we touch palm to palm, we make a heart connection. Parents reach for their child's hand for security and bonding. Children reach for a parent's hand for the same reasons. In fact, a hand reaches out to greet us from the first moment we arrive on the planet. Lovers hold hands in a closeness that only holding hands can easily express. Business men and women shake hands in greeting and, for that brief moment, a connection is made in friendship.

In the age of high technology, human touch is important. Let us hold on to the bond of friendship through the touch of human hands. Make a heartfelt connection with every hand you touch.

The Healing Energy of Touch

TOUCH · TOUCH · TOUCH · TOUCH · TOUCH · TOUCH · TOUCH · TOUCH · TOUCH · TOUCH

A hug, a pat on the back, or a touch of the hand are signs of friendship we often do casually and naturally. That's how we transfer goodwill, good intentions, happiness and joy from one person to another. It's a simple act of exchanging energy. The human animal needs human touch—not necessarily skin touching skin, but an exchange of human energy. However, the simple act of exchanging energy may not be so simple after all.

Healers far and wide, who see energy as auras pulsating throughout the body, harness the power of touch to do their healing work. The unmistakable truth is we all have the healing power of touch. And what the healers also tell us is that the *intention* to heal through touch is reciprocal, meaning we, ourselves, benefit as well from the exchange.

When the time is right, give someone a hug, a pat on the back or a touch of the hand to let that person know you care. Feel the energy.

Loosen Up!

Fashion notwithstanding, clothes serve a definite purpose particularly if you live where temperatures dip below freezing. But no one ever said that clothes have to serve as a straitjacket. One of the first things I teach in my stress management classes is to loosen any tight-fitting clothing.

Check your clothing right now. Are you comfortable? Does anything feel tight? Can you unbutton the top button or loosen your tie? Can you kick off your shoes? Tight-fitting clothes tend to make you feel uptight. The feel of fabric against your skin should be a pleasurable experience.

Here is an idea. Fridays are considered casual days at the worksite, but why not take the sting out of Mondays and make them "loosen up day." Put on some silk underwear and undo the top button of your shirt. Get comfortable and loosen up.

Barefoot and Fancy Free

TOUCH · TOUCH · TOUCH · TOUCH · TOUCH · TOUCH · TOUCH · TOUCH · TOUCH · TOUCH

O h, the freedom of bare feet. To feel the softness of carpet, the pleasure of moss and grass, the firmness of concrete or the cool touch of slate is an exploration into the unknown. Shoes imprison the feet. When was the last time you intentionally walked barefoot through freshly mown grass? Even if it was yesterday, you are overdue for another journey.

As kids, we could easily forget to put our shoes on. Now that we are older and putting on shoes is as routine as brushing our teeth, it's time to declare independence! Kick off your shoes and explore the world through your feet and toes—grass, concrete, wood floors, carpet, even mud. Don't worry about feeling foolish (the feet have no ego), that's the whole idea.

Hot Nights, Cool Breeze

"**D**id you feel that?" my grandmother asks.

"What?" I want to know.

"Did you feel that slight breeze?" she continues. The beads of sweat on my forehead, flooding my eyebrows, distracts my attention from the whisper of relief she feels.

I am sitting with my grandparents on the front porch of their tiny house. It's about a half hour past sunset, and the sky is still light. The heat is oppressive. For as hot as it is outside, it's even hotter inside. So we sit outside, eyes closed, waiting for the relief of night and the chance of a cool breeze.

"Here it comes again. Close your eyes and feel," she instructs. Sure enough I do. I feel the essence of a cool breeze on my forehead, cheeks and bare shoulders.

On the hottest of nights you can feel a breeze, one that touches your skin and carries the heat away; all you have to do is sit still and feel.

Next time the weather is hot and muggy, step outside for a moment to feel the slightest of breezes. Then wait again. The next breeze is about to begin. Be patient.

A Shower and Shave

S ometime between the first days of spring and the last days of summer, our bodies change and the wish to be grown-up is fully realized. What was once an experiment in the bathroom with a razor blade and a few stray whiskers is now simply routine. In fact, so quick are we to shower and shave that we often forget to enjoy that softness of skin we rushed so quickly to achieve.

The pulsation of hot beads of water against the skin, a massage of sorts, is heavenly. Water makes a great lubricant to shave (face or legs), which is a bonus of taking a shower. The stroke of softness against the skin after the razor has done its work is heavenly, too. Next time you shave in the shower, give yourself a few extra moments to enjoy a return to the springtime of your youth.

A Thousand Grains of Sand

A barefoot walk on the beach is such a tempting delight. To feel the grains of sand squish through your toes with each step is a call to simpler times. But the hands enjoy sand as well. If you watch beachgoers, it is common to see them fill their cupped hands and slowly let the brown, white, pink or black granules cascade back to the source—each grain making contact with the skin as it falls. The next time you find yourself at the beach, be it the ocean or the banks of a river, fill your hands with sand. Then let the sand sift slowly through your fingers. It is said that one hand can hold as many as a thousand grains of sand. Who's counting?

Keep Those Raindrops Falling on My Face

TOUCH · TOUCH · TOUCH · TOUCH · TOUCH · TOUCH · TOUCH · TOUCH · TOUCH · TOUCH

The first reaction to an encounter with rain is anything but calm. Out come the umbrellas, raincoats and hats to prevent us from experiencing what happened to the wicked witch of the west—a soggy meltdown.

But if we could step outside our egos for a moment, perhaps we might enjoy those precious raindrops. To feel rain, from a light mist to heavy drops, on the face is cleansing. Try this. When you feel down in the dumps about some problem or issue, and Mother Nature is having a good cry as well, step outside and lift your face to the heavens. Let the rain symbolically wash away your worries. You may even find yourself singing in the rain.

The Good Earth

The word *human* comes from the root *humus,* which means "of the earth." To hold rich, dark, moist soil in the palm of the hand is a clarion call to the roots of humanity. Nowhere is this more likely to happen than in the garden.

Many people cite gardening as a most pleasurable and relaxing hobby. They will often confide that the touch of soil is the most fulfilling. Even city dwellers who cultivate their geraniums in flower boxes dig their fingers into the dirt to make that primordial connection. Of course, there is more to gardening than moist soil, but it all starts there. Making contact with the plant's roots, leaves and buds is essential, too. The end result: a flower blossom, edible fruit, vegetable or herb to remind us of how good the earth really is. So reach out and touch the earth today.

Sun Kisses and Vitamin D

As a young boy, I was told freckles were the result of where the sun kissed you. I had hundreds of freckles so I figured the sun *really* liked me. I knew then what I have come to appreciate now: feeling the warmth of the sun on your face, or anywhere on your body, feels great, in moderate amounts, of course. I later learned that the body uses sunlight to make vitamin D, an essential nutrient. Has the sun kissed you today?

Get Fleeced!

An expression in the Scandinavian countries translates roughly as, "There is no such thing as bad weather, only bad clothing!" They should know. It gets mighty cold up there near the Arctic Circle.

So what is the fabric of choice by those in the know? Fleece! Years ago fleece meant wool, but today several synthetics serve well in its place. The touch can best be described in one word: *soft.* Whereas wool tends to be scratchy, synthetic fleece is nothing less than cozy. If you have not discovered fleece (in all its many brand names), you are missing out on one of life's finer luxuries. Fleece coats, blankets, sweatpants, shirts, socks and hats. Take some advice from the Nordic folks and get fleeced.

The Longest Kiss

Let's face it, lips are one of the greatest human features. They curve to smile, they move to talk, they pucker to kiss. Oh, to feel the lips of your lover against yours, to move two sets of lips in unison as if dancing on a stage, to have lips meet and connect is to know one of the greatest feelings on earth. Granted, there are many types of kisses, but the passionate kiss is by far the best because it is only reserved for that special person. The touch of moist lips against yours is undeniably one of the greatest pleasures ever known. Don't forget to breathe!

Only Soft Edges

T he human hand likes a soft, smooth object such as a tumbled stone to touch and hold. An object of such character is pleasing to the skin and to the mind as well.

Tumbled stones of rose quartz, lapis lazuli, turquoise, agate or malachite go through a process where, through friction, resistance and the passage of water, the rough edges are smoothed and the stones radiate the natural colors in all their glory. There is a symbolic message here. We, too, go through life meeting resistance and friction. If we can learn from our experiences then we, like the tumbled stone, can become soft and colorful.

If you should not happen to have a tumbled stone or two to roll around in your hand, you can pick them up along riverbanks, the shores of large bodies of water or, for a very small price, at a neighborhood nature store. Leave some stones around your home and office. When tension rises, reach for a few stones, close your eyes and maneuver the stones between your fingers and palm. The relaxing message you give your skin and mind is one and the same.

Pussy Willows and Cattails

Mother Nature holds many strange and wonderful textures in her purse. Among the most pleasing are the buds, leaves and new growth of flora with the first signs of spring. Here is a challenge. Plan a walk in the woods in the spring or summer and see the world through your fingers rather than your eyes. If you were to walk with a child, two of the first things he or she would gravitate toward are pussy willows and cattails because they are soft and fuzzy—nature's magnets to human hands. If you can, set out to find some pussy willows and cattails, then bring some home and place them in a vase of water in the kitchen. Can you describe in rich detail what you feel—as if touching them for the first time?

Going with the Grain

A friend of mine who builds furniture explained to me, "You don't touch wood, you caress it." The expression "knock on wood" may extend a sense of hope in a moment of doubt, but have you ever truly felt the grain of wood before it is stained and finished? Extremely smooth to the touch, the grain of finely sanded wood is alluring. The wood's even texture seems to communicate with the fine lines etched in our fingertips. The result is heavenly. Once finely sanded, wood grain—whether it be oak, pine, ash, maple, cherry or cedar—is a delight only the hands may know.

Wood is a grounding element. Trees, with their roots deep in the ground, portray a sense of stability and security. Wood, too, conveys this essence. It is said that wooden instruments like the violin and cello create a better resonance with age. In a sense, the essence of the tree lives long after the wood has been cut. Stop in at a furniture

177

store and observe people as they walk by the wood furniture. Unlike metal furniture, they cannot keep from caressing the grain. Most likely you will reach out and touch, too.

The Big Wave

There's something special about moving water. Take body surfing, for example. Like the wave that rises and falls, so too does the body's level of tension and relaxation, from the anticipation to the "ahh" when the tail of the wave delivers you to the shore. One ride is never enough, so you go back out in search of the next wave to ride. In that moment of motion, in the moment of suspended force, there is a sense of peace only the body knows. My favorite place to body surf is on the north beach of Kauai. But when I can't get to the ocean, I feel the rush of water against my skin while swimming at the local recreation center. You can too. Surf's up!

A Friendly Hug

TOUCH • TOUCH • TOUCH • TOUCH • TOUCH • TOUCH • TOUCH • TOUCH • TOUCH • TOUCH

As a rule, Americans don't touch. Europeans, Middle Easterners—now these people touch. They hug, they kiss (on both cheeks, no less) and then they touch some more. It's their culture. We Americans are getting better, but we have a way to go. With the Puritan and Victorian influences somewhat behind us, we are becoming better at public displays of affection. Which leads us to the hug phenomena.

Did you ever notice the different types of hugs?

- The air hug (don't mess up the makeup)
- The one-arm hug (an acquaintance building to a friendship)
- The high-five hug (just for athletes)
- The A-frame hug (don't get too close)
- The bear hug (when you really want to say hi)
- The loving hug (for that extra special someone)

With rare exception, hugs are therapeutic. They provide a sense of belonging, acceptance and friendship. They also bring security and trust—all that from a brief embrace. Forced hugs don't work. But a friendly hug does wonders for both body and soul, for both people involved. Should you feel so inspired, give somebody a heartfelt hug today.

Just a Little Secret

F reedom! We all want it. We all crave it. We miss it when we are denied it, and we often take it for granted when have too much of it. We even break rules in the name of freedom. Some rules are more cultural, others quite personal. Some rules, however, can be broken and no one ever knows. Such is the rule with underwear.

There is no law that says you have to wear underwear (all the time). This can be your little secret. The (occasional) freedom feels wonderful and gives a whole new meaning to the concept of "casual day." Some precautions are necessary, so take heed. And should the topic ever come up about boxers or briefs, you can say "both" or you can just smile.

The Garden of Eden

A lthough we may never know exactly what happened in the garden that auspicious day, I think we can safely assume that at some point Adam and Eve fell in love. The difference between sex and making love is the intention. More than just a physical release, the art of lovemaking is ecstatic arousal where receiving pleasure (and ultimately relaxation) is only exceeded by giving pleasure to your partner. Surely more than one sense is involved in this exchange, but suffice to say that the sense of touch has top billing. Of course the sensation is enhanced with the subtleties of massage oil, water or perhaps even a soft feather. The art of lovemaking is, by all accounts, a sacred ritual. Make each occasion a blessed event.

Kneading a Helping Hand

O kay! So you find yourself bored with absolutely nothing to do on a Saturday or Sunday, and the wild idea strikes to make bread—by hand. Fresh-baked bread. Martha Stewart will never tell you this, but baking bread is really a therapy session in disguise.

You comb through the kitchen, and sure enough you have all the ingredients. So, after mixing the flour and eggs and yeast (and whatever else you want to add: olives, herbs, fruit or nuts) and placing plenty of flour on the counter, now comes the fun part. Invoking the spirit of Freud, Jung or Maslow (take your pick), you begin to knead the dough. Feel the damp flour concoction ooze through your fingers as you take a deep breath. Exhale and release! Pull the dough back toward you and grab a big wad between your fingers and thumbs. Squeeze, breathe, release! Repeat. Continue this for a good twenty minutes. Then throw the dough in a bread pan, let it rise, punch it down once more before you place your beloved masterpiece in the oven and wait for it to turn golden brown. Now *this* is relaxation therapy.

An Intense Cleansing Heat

Scandinavians long ago discovered that moist heat enhances the skin's breathing capacity and rejuvenates the body in a unique cleansing action. Moist heat opens the skin's pores and coaxes toxins, residues and chemicals out. Moreover, the heat of a sauna brings blood to the skin's surface, allowing for a relaxing effect of the muscle tissues.

Once on a trip to Norway, I partook in the ritual of a sauna in the dark of winter. Heat never felt so good. Custom then followed to exit the hot shed and plunge into a freezing cold pond. Brrr! You don't have to go to Norway to take a sauna; the nearest gym or hotel will do. But take my advice: Skip the icy plunge!

Water Paradise

I magine the ultimate private getaway. Here's how to achieve pure relaxation. Today's flotation tanks are long and shallow (just four to six inches deep), allowing you to float effortlessly on your back. The water is rich in salt, allowing even the heaviest person to achieve a sense of accomplishment. The sense of touch (warm water on skin) is the only sense activated. Stimulation to all other senses is nil, kind of like being back in the womb. And, oh, is it relaxing. Like a massage, you just don't want it to end. I highly recommend it. If you cannot find a place that offers flotation tank services, you can achieve a similar sensation in a crowded pool using a pull-buoy between your legs to keep yourself afloat.

Butterfly Kisses

Actor Kevin Costner gently flickered his eyelashes on the cherub cheek of his young daughter in a movie. She giggled. Then the gossamer wings of her long eyelashes landed on his cheek, and the butterfly kiss was complete.

Butterfly kisses are a cute way of being approachable yet somewhat reserved, intimate yet cordial with someone you trust and love. Life imitates nature and the cycle is complete. It is a neat sensation to feel the gentle wisp of hair and air on your cheek or brow. Save this one for close family members, like young children and spouses. I guarantee you will become a fan of butterflies and butterfly kisses.

Thank You, Mr. Jacuzzi

Hydrotherapy, the practice of submerging oneself into circulating hot water to relax, dates back to ancient Greece. In fact, native peoples of all cultures quickly discovered the healing effects of thermal pools and revered them as sacred sites. Natural pools of hot spring water with effervescent air bubbles rising to the surface, the result of geothermal activity, were great. Hot water drew blood to the extremities. Muscles, once tense, became more pliant as they filled with blood.

But not everybody could travel to special places to sink into the healing waters. So about fifty years ago, Candidio Jacuzzi came up with the idea for a hot spring in the backyard. He called it the "bubbly bath," but it now bears his own name.

To sit comfortably in a hot tub on a cool night and feel thousands of air bubbles glide past your skin as they float to the surface is a

189

birthright for everyone (it's even better without a swimsuit). The combination of hot soothing water with fizzing bubbles in contrast to a cool evening breeze is the epitome of relaxation. Should you not happen to have your own Jacuzzi, call a friend who does and subtly invite yourself over. Don't forget the beverages.

Finally, a Massage!

TOUCH · TOUCH · TOUCH · TOUCH · TOUCH · TOUCH · TOUCH · TOUCH · TOUCH · TOUCH

Muscle tension is the number one symptom of stress. Nervous tension starts, builds and accumulates in the muscle tissues and, over time, can cause real problems with the body's structural alignment and posture. The (best) remedy: a full-body massage. Aside from the fact that humans need touch and get far too little of it, bodywork, from Swedish massage and shiatsu to myofascial release and rolfing, offers a means to come back to balance, and it feels so good.

If you have never had a professional massage, you're missing one of the finer experiences in life. Certified massage therapists are well trained to work the tension out of your muscles and bring you to a place of calm. How do you pick a massage therapist? Ask around. Get a recommendation from a friend. Costs vary around the country, but there is no doubt you will find that it's a wonderful investment again and again and again.

SIX

Relaxing Through the Divine Sense

Some experiences promote such a sense of awe, wonder, gratitude and calm that they simply cannot be identified with just one of the five senses. In fact, perhaps it is best said that these experiences cannot even be put into words. In many cases these special moments, these mystical happenings, tap into all five of the body's senses plus one more. I refer to a power greater than sight, sound, touch, taste and smell—the divine sense. It is in all of us.

Stress is often defined as a perceived disconnection from our divine source. Although we never are truly disconnected or separated from

God, moments of chaos and catastrophe may make it seem as if we are. But for every stressful moment in which we mistakenly believe that we have been divinely abandoned, there are a multitude of moments that remind us that we are never alone. Psychologist Abraham Maslow called these sensations "peak experiences," where we know, if only for a brief moment, that we are truly one with God. I prefer the term "holy moments," brief, but powerful mystical experiences in which we use our divine sense to know that, however insignificant we may seem in the ever-expanding universe, we are an *essential* part of it all.

How can the divine sense best be explained? As poet Maya Angelou says in her book *Wouldn't Take Nothing for My Journey Now,* "I believe that Spirit is one and everywhere present. That it never leaves me. That in my ignorance, I may withdraw from it, but I can realize its presence the instant I return to my senses." The divine sense is a conscious recognition that we are always in the presence of God, however we conceive this to be.

The graceful flight of a monarch butterfly. Miles of pink and orange clouds at sunset. The smile on the face of a young child. The divine sense can be realized through all the five senses, but it doesn't stop there. Our divine connection is made manifest through our sense of humor, our sense of imagination and creativity, our sense of intuition and our sense of compassion. I call these senses the muscles of the soul.

In addition to realizing our divine connection, these senses help us transcend the roadblocks that stress puts in front of us. It is interesting to note that when I ask my students this question, "What divine experiences bring peace?" the answers seem to fall into two categories: Either being completely alone with God (usually in nature), or in the company of friends, with the underlying assumption that the face of God can be found on every human face.

Coming to a sense of calm through the divine sense is a very personal undertaking. It is fair to say that no two of these experiences are alike. Reflect for a moment on what you would include to remind yourself of and to cultivate your own personal sense of the divine in everyday life.

Holy Moments

Spotting a bald eagle flying overhead. Experiencing the birth of a child. Falling in love. Watching a magnificent sunset. A holy moment is any experience you have when you feel you are one with God.

Holy moments are times when the walls of the ego are lowered so that we can gain a clear picture of our divine connection. Some people call it a spiritual orgasm. For me it was hugging a dolphin on a trip to Florida (an unexpected hug). For a friend it was getting cancer, so she could begin to live her life the way she really wanted.

We are cultured to think that these special moments are rare, but in truth they don't have to be. What has been your most significant holy moment so far? Unlike going to a movie, you cannot actually drive to a holy moment. But you can prepare for one. Preparing takes place in the mind, through acceptance, humbleness and love.

Back to Nature

The ocean breeze in the morning. The mountain air before a storm. The dew on the grass. The mist in the hills. The elk at sunset. We have heard it all before—but we need constant reminding. We are part of nature, and we are called to be a part of nature regularly.

In the velocity of life, it is easy to remain confined in our cars, offices, homes and minds—so that we rarely get intimate with the elements. The end result is a feeling of alienation, a feeling that does nothing to promote relaxation.

But nature coaxes us outside in her own way. The forces of nature are compelling and dynamic, but they are also subtle. Find a quiet place, perhaps by a tree, and sit for a while. Soak it all in.

The Wild Fandango

Line dancing in Nashville, funking the blues in Chicago, clogging in upstate New York, tap dancing in L.A. or performing modern dance in St. Louis. When you dance without inhibition, you set your spirit free and this is totally relaxing. The music pulsates, the air is electric, the lights are dim and you are one with the music.

Dance really can do this to you. To move freely to the vibrations of music, or in syncopated rhythm with a partner, is one of humankind's greatest pleasures. Not merely one sense is turned on, they all are. But there is something more going on. You are transformed—in your body and out of your body at the same time. The beauty of dancing is you don't have to leave the house to do it. Just pull the blinds, crank up the music and hit the floor smiling (like Tom Cruise in *Risky Business*).

Not Just a Coincidence

There you are sitting at your desk, thinking about an old college chum whom you haven't heard from in years, and just as you pick up the phone to make a call, it rings and guess who? Coincidence?

You awaken from a sound sleep but recall a vivid dream in which you meet a man with a mustache who negotiates a winning business deal. The next day at work you see the man from your dreams, someone you know you have never seen before. Coincidence?

When two seemingly random events occur and we find meaning, it's enough to give you goose bumps. We call this synchronicity, and what it really means is that there is a divine plan to the universe. I believe it was Dr. Bernie Siegel who once said, "A coincidence is God's way of remaining anonymous." When you start looking for synchronicity you'll see more of it. A coincidence is a peek at the divine game plan.

Moving On

The human journey can be a wonderful voyage, filled with terrific experiences, but even the best vacations can have upsets. Such is life. And although we are told time and time again to lighten our load, the baggage we carry around for security can be so heavy, it makes the human journey unbearable. The baggage I am referring to is emotional baggage, comprised primarily of unresolved issues of stress. Inside the bags may be anger (the fight emotion) and fear (the flight emotion).

"Moving on" is an expression meaning to let go of any thoughts, feelings, attitudes, perceptions, opinions and beliefs that no longer serve us. These are the ones that hold us back. More often than not, the means to move on is to forgive. Remember, when you forgive someone, you don't do it for them, you do it for yourself so you can move on.

Is there an issue waiting to be resolved? Is there a person you need to forgive so you can move on? Unpack those bags. The time is now.

Be Creative!

C reativity is a combination of right-brain imagination and left-brain organization. Creativity is not a gift for a chosen few. It is a birthright for everyone.

The creative muscle gets flexed with hobbies: photography, gardening, cooking, drawing, designing Web pages, building sandcastles, playing with pets, you name it. It is not what you do that counts, but simply engaging in the act that matters. In the field of health psychology this is known as being a co-creator (with God as your partner, of course). Hobbies are widely known to promote relaxation because they take you out of a chaotic world and place you in a more controlled setting, with you at the controls. Hobbies also become the stepping-stone in the stream of a career change. So how do you express your creativity? It's always time for a new project.

Tiny Bubbles

Blowing bubbles. Remember doing this as a kid? Blowing bubbles is an activity which definitely places you in the present moment. You cannot think of stock markets, staff meetings, traffic jams or grocery shopping when you are blowing bubbles.

To blow a bubble, or series of bubbles, with each one carrying a rainbow, is to be engaged in the present moment and nothing could be more divine.

So the next time you're near a local drug store, stop in and pick up a bottle of bubble mix. Then when the pressures of life seem to get you down, walk outside, take a seat on the steps of your porch or patio, open the lid, pull out the ring, pucker up and blow. Watch your cares and worries fade, as the bubbles themselves take flight and fly away.

Lending a Helping Hand

DIVINE · DIVINE · DIVINE · DIVINE · DIVINE · DIVINE · DIVINE · DIVINE · DIVINE · DIVINE

At some point in our lives we realize that to be human means to serve others, to lend a helping hand. To be of service to those who need assistance is one of the greatest gifts we can give. But true service is not a one-way street, for when we make ourselves available, we benefit as well. Giving and receiving becomes one. Sometimes the time we can be most helpful is when we feel as if we ourselves are at rock bottom. Lending a helping hand, when our own hands are cut, scraped and bruised from our own stress, shows we are real people, not saints.

What can you do to lend a helping hand? Volunteer at a soup kitchen. Visit a nursing home with your dog. Offer to baby-sit for a friend. There is no shortage of ways to open your heart.

Time for a Potluck Supper

There are times when we want to be alone, and times when it's so important to be with friends. Friends are those people who love and accept you for who you are. They're there for you when the chips are down and to share in life's glories. We are lucky if three or four people in our lives fall into the category of true friend.

There is a custom in the South Pacific where, for no reason whatsoever, people congregate to celebrate life. Really it's a celebration of friendships. The word is spread to come for dinner and bring something to share. Sounds like a potluck supper to me. Potlucks are great because the pressure is off to make a whole meal; everybody shares in the responsibilities, and that's the meaning of friendship anyway.

So pick a day, maybe even tonight. Call your friends and invite them over. If you really want to add some variety, create a theme to go with the potluck dinner (a tie party, a hat party, a CD party, a photo album party, a South Pacific party. It's time to celebrate life! It's time to celebrate friendship!

Finding the Treasure with the Map

We tend to think of inner peace as a brief moment in time, the calm between storms. But in the bigger picture, inner peace is a lifelong process in our search for meaningful purpose. Unsure of your direction? Let's make a treasure map. Here's how:

First make a list of goals that you really want to accomplish (personal, professional or both). Next, go around the house and collect all the magazines you can find. While you're doing this, pick up a pair of scissors and glue or tape, as well as a large piece of white paper. Then go through the magazines looking for photos, words, phrases, images of things that support your life mission through these goals. Begin to cut and paste these onto the paper. Try to fill in all the spaces before you finish. Then hang the map in a place where you can see it regularly. Let your unconscious mind do the rest.

Making a Pilgrimage

Do you have a calling to go somewhere? Perhaps the Sistine Chapel awaits your visit. Maybe Jerusalem is calling to you. Perhaps it's the Caribbean or maybe New Zealand. Have you thought about it? Where is your mecca?

Ageless wisdom tells us we have to leave home on a journey to explore new landscapes, cultures and experiences that could not be accomplished at home. Countless fairy tales foretell of pilgrimages that heroes must take to become full adults.

In truth, the journey is the destination. The actual "end point" is a vehicle for change and growth. So we go and we grow, and then we come home and we share what we experienced and learned. A pilgrimage—and there are many in one lifetime—is a sacred rite of passage, and through it all we are transformed. Where does your spirit call you? Where are you going today?

Encore! Encore!

The usher takes you to your seat and you greet the people next to you. At that moment the anticipation begins. A Broadway play, a rock concert, a local stage production, music under the stars. Every seat is taken. Standing room only. The lights dim, the show starts and all eyes look forward to the first stage entrance.

To be in a crowd of people enjoying a stage production is liberating, especially when the final applause begins. Thousands of people clapping, cheering, showing their enthusiasm and appreciation, with beams of energy emanating from each face and heart. To share this feeling of oneness with everyone who has experienced the magic of the moment is akin to feeling "one with the universe." The performers come back on stage and they give an encore to end all encores. You are in absolute heaven. So if you have not experienced the exchange between artist and audience, check your local paper for listings of events and get tickets for the big show.

Parking Angels

Y ou get out of your meeting late, only to find when you get to your car that the gas tank is nearly empty. Your next meeting is across town and already you're behind schedule. In what seems like hours, but is really only minutes, the tank is filled and you are on your way. But you're still late. A quick glance reveals that parking is going to be a problem. Your heart starts pounding, blood pressure rises, the stress response has kicked in. But as luck would have it, a car pulls out of a choice parking spot in front of you, and you slide right in. Praise be to the parking angels! They heard the call. Of course it might have helped if you had given them a little more warning, but it worked out. It always does. Next time you're running late, or perhaps just having a hard time finding a place to park your car, give the parking angels a call.

Parking angels are really time managers. Now remember, if they don't answer your immediate call for an easy parking space, remind yourself that they are still working behind the scenes—delaying your schedule for some yet-to-be-determined reason.

Turn Off the Alarm Clock

DIVINE · DIVINE · DIVINE · DIVINE · DIVINE · DIVINE · DIVINE · DIVINE · DIVINE · DIVINE

What could be more divine than a good night's sleep? We spend as much as a third of our lives unconscious. At least we can be comfortable in this state, right? Sleep is one of those conditions where, when it's good, you don't really notice, but when it's bad, it affects everything you do the next day. Some studies suggest that 30 percent of the American population suffers from insomnia. If it's not insomnia, it might be a sick child, bladder problems, howling winds or some other disturbance. Good sleep really is divine.

Would an extra hour of sleep make a difference? It couldn't hurt. Here's an idea. To insure that the alarm clock is not programmed to wake you up on the weekends, unplug it. To ensure quality sleep, avoid eating rich foods late at night and listen to some pleasing music before closing your eyes.

If you find yourself sleep-deprived, try taking some valerian or melatonin, cut back on the caffeine or go for a short walk before bed to ease you in the direction of slumberland.

The Healing Power of Love

Nothing brings hearts and souls together like love. Love is truly the greatest healing force in the world. We need love to survive, for without it we die. Love is the one thing that when we give it, we get it back ten-fold. Ask any person what brings a sense of calm to the spirit and undoubtedly you will hear the word *love*. Love is a universal truth we can count on, and for love to do its work, it must be shared.

There are many shades of colors in love's rainbow to share: faith, humor, optimism, humbleness, courage, patience, forgiveness and compassion, to name a few. The healing power of love can occur in moments, such a phone call to a friend, a random act of kindness, a hug or a handshake. The healing power of love begins with an open heart. Try this today: Engage in a random act of kindness. Then see what happens. See how you feel inside.

214

Poetry in Motion

Reading poetry is an invitation to take a healthy pause in our fast-paced lives and catch our breath. To read poetry, and read it well, you must slow down and study the words. The added benefit of reading a poem is the rhyme, for rhymes suggest order in a seemingly chaotic world. When you read a poem, pause after the first line and reflect on it for a moment. What does it mean to you? It is suggested that once you read a selected poem, read it again, even slower this time. As Robert Frost once said after reading one of his own, "Now I'm going to read it again, so pay attention."

Do you write poems? Writing poems is an act of grace as well. And to read a poem that has just come off your own pen is again a reminder to pause and celebrate life.

The Last Good-bye

"Sometimes letting go means finally saying good-bye," said Becky, one of my graduate students. She was referring to the death of her husband, a man whom she deeply loved and had been married to for two decades. As she recounted to me, he had died of cancer a couple of years before. She was still grieving. She decided to write him a letter and wish him a final farewell, not to forget about him, but to let him go so she could move on with her life. The next week in class she told me the letter was more like a book. She even mailed it!

I saw Becky a year later. She was jubilant. No longer was she carrying the weight of her husband on her shoulders. It was at that time she mentioned that saying good-bye had finally brought her peace. Is there someone whom you might care to write a letter to, which will bring peace to your heart?

A Whole New World to Explore

To experience a universe below the surface of the water, to scuba dive among life forms unimaginable, to glide by inconceivably intricate coral structures and witness majestic water colors is to know sublime exhilaration. The combination of the feel of the water with the stunning visual stimulation is unparalleled. Snorkeling ranks a close second. Sight but no sound, except the noise of your own breath, provides a mysterious presence that is difficult to put into words.

The world may have seven seas, but there is no limit to the bodies of water begging to be explored. Not certified, you say. Well, it's not hard to remedy that situation. Call your local recreation department to find out when the next scuba class is being held. Life under the sea will change yours.

Riding the Wind

Any time you can move faster than your two feet will allow, and feel the rush of wind on your face, the spirit rejoices: Rollerblading, downhill skiing, sailing, airplane gliding, most definitely hot-air ballooning. To harness the power of movement is exhilarating. And the moment you finish, you want to do it again.

You don't need to have your feet off the ground to allow your spirit to soar, but it helps. So if you're looking for a way to get out of the emotional rut of everyday living, hoist your sails and ride the wind—the breath of Mother Earth. If these opportunities are not readily available, try flying a kite. Your spirit will soar.

A River Runs Through It, Really!

DIVINE · DIVINE · DIVINE · DIVINE · DIVINE · DIVINE · DIVINE · DIVINE · DIVINE · DIVINE

There is a picture postcard on my cousin's office door of two men fly-fishing in a stream, having a good old time. Beneath the photo is the caption, "Stress-Management Seminar." Sometimes when I call cousin Scott at work, I'm told he's in stress-management training. Then I know exactly what coping skill he's practicing—fly-fishing.

Many friends and colleagues who fish tell me catching a fish isn't really the goal. The goal is just getting outside—away from the office. While communing with nature sets the stage for this divine experience, the exhilaration is in the freedom and inaccessibility to the "real world." To catch a fish is just icing on the cake. Most people throw back what they catch anyway. And when they come home and tell you a fish story—about the one that got away—know that it was a very successful seminar. Next time, ask if you can join them.

Try Turning the TV Off Tonight

T o sit in front of the television may seem like a relaxing way to spend the evening, but in truth it can suck the life energy out of you. Television can be addictive, for what usually starts out as watching a half-hour sitcom ends up being another wasted night in front of the boob tube—every night.

So rather than be passively entertained with someone else's creativity (or lack thereof), try turning off the television one night a week and forcing yourself to do something else. Listen to music. Play that instrument you haven't touched in months. Pull out a cookbook and whip up something fantastic. You will be surprised how creative you become and how simple your life will be.

The One That Got Away

S o you're driving a little faster than the law allows and, wouldn't you know it, your rearview mirror reveals red-and-blue flashing lights coming your way. You pull over and so does the police officer. He gets out and walks toward your car. You roll down your window and give one of those guilty-but-humble smiles.

The cop takes your license and registration and walks back to check them out. You sit in your car, humiliated. In what seems like hours, the cop finally comes back and says, "You were speeding, but I'm only going to give you a warning this time." You want to kiss his hand, but instead you simply say thanks, close your eyes and take a deep breath. To be sure, being stopped by a policeman is not a calming experience, but on those occasions where we are let off the hook, the moment of stress transforms to instant relief. Be on the lookout for blessings that begin as curses.

From a Trot to a Gallop

The first thing you want to do is pet the horse, just to touch it and make contact. You smell the leather saddle, the hay in the barn, and you breathe a long sigh, having waited for this moment, just the two of you. Then your hand slides over the smooth leather of the saddle. You hoist yourself up and now you are one with the horse. After a few words of encouragement (to yourself, not the horse), you're off. With your hands on the reins, you turn the horse around and head out to the pasture. With a gentle kick of your heels, the body beneath you moves into a gallop and you move in rhythm to the horse's body. This is freedom and it is wild.

Fantasies of the wild West abound—to be free on a horse, galloping with the wind in your hair. Have you ever been on a horse? It really is a neat experience. And whether you get a chance to gallop or merely go on a trail ride, the opportunity calls you. Happy trails!

It's Positively Grand!

To stand on the precipice of the Grand Canyon and look for miles into the deep gorge carved by the Colorado River is inspiring: the sight of the North Rim, the South Rim, the colors of the rock, the sky, the painted desert. The aroma of the ponderosa pine and the smell of dry, cool air fill the senses. No words can describe the beauty.

To stand facing the Grand Tetons is nothing less than a spiritual moment. The jagged peaks remind one of a medieval time of kings, queens, knights, dragons and fairytale romance.

This is nature like nothing else. These are my two favorite sacred sites. To be sure, there are hundreds of other places in the world that would electrify every aspect of your mind, body and spirit. Where are yours?

Grab Your Helmet and Go

Do you have a bike? Good! Then you know just how great it is to hop on the seat and take off. Freedom. First you pedal, then you coast, then you find a comfortable rhythm—a metaphor for life. So you coast, and you smile, and you think, gosh, this is great. Whether you have a road bike, trail bike or mountain bike, the combined motion of two wheels and scenery is unbeatable. You don't have a bike you say? Well, you can easily rent one at any bike store, or perhaps you can borrow one from a friend. But don't pass up an opportunity to coast wherever two wheels can take you. Don't forget your helmet!

The Blue Lagoon

Aqua-blue water. Is there nothing more calm than this? Throw in some salt air, a sandy beach, a few palm trees, lots of sunshine and you're in heaven. The Virgin Islands, the Florida Keys, the Hawaiian Islands, Cancun and the entire Caribbean are beckoning you to visit and relax. But it's not just the distinctive color of the water and the sunshine. It's the total package that, together with you, creates paradise. Anyone who has ever gone to a blue-lagoon paradise comes back a changed person. There is serenity in their eyes, a smile on their face, that lasts long after they have arrived back home. Everyone should go at least once to a blue lagoon. Can you hear the call?

Epilogue

Every day we are invited to participate fully in life, yet it is not uncommon to let the days slip by, often taking each moment for granted, or worse, complaining about how bad life can be. Rather than feeling energized by our sensations, we feel drained. Life, however, is a balance of good and bad experiences; it was never meant to be dismal. It is up to each and every one of us to seek the balance, find the good and reach a state of calm. Remember, no one is going to do it for you. May your journey be filled with many blessings.

Other Great Books on Relaxation

Carlson, Richard. *Don't Sweat the Small Stuff . . . and It's All Small Stuff.* New York: Hyperion Books, 1997.

Kabat-Zinn, Jon. *Wherever You Go, There You Are.* New York: Hyperion Books, 1994.

Roberts, Elizabeth, and Elias Amidon. *Earth Prayers.* San Francisco: HarperCollins, 1988.

—————. *Life Prayers.* San Francisco: HarperCollins, 1993.

Seaward, Brian Luke. *Stand Like Mountain, Flow Like Water.* Deerfield Beach, Fla.: Health Communications, Inc., 1997.

—————. *Stressed Is Desserts Spelled Backward.* Berkeley, Calif.: Conari Press, 1999.

Watterson, Bill. *The Essential Calvin & Hobbes.* Kansas City, Mo.: Andrews & McMeel, 1988.

—————. *The Indispensable Calvin & Hobbes.* Kansas City, Mo.: Andrews & McMeel, 1990.

————. *The Authoritative Calvin & Hobbes.* Kansas City, Mo.: Andrews & McMeel, 1992.

————. *The Days Are Just Packed: A Calvin & Hobbes Collection.* Kansas City, Mo.: Andrews & McMeel, 1993.

————. *Homicidal Psycho Jungle Cat: A Calvin & Hobbes Collection.* Kansas City, Mo.: Andrews & McMeel, 1994.

————. *The Calvin & Hobbes Tenth Anniversary Edition.* Kansas City, Mo.: Andrews & McMeel, 1995.

————. *It's a Magical World: A Calvin & Hobbes Collection.* Kansas City, Mo.: Andrews & McMeel, 1996.

————. *There's Treasure Everywhere: A Calvin & Hobbes Collection.* Kansas City, Mo.: Andrews & McMeel, 1996.

Music for Relaxation

I'm often asked by friends and acquaintances for some good recommendations for relaxing music. Here are some of my favorite acoustic instrumental music, listed by instrument (artist and CD title); enjoy:

Piano

- Jim Wilson: *Northern Seascape*
- Danny Wright: *Phantasys*
- Robin Spielberg: *In the Arms of the Wind*
- Tom Barabas: *Sedona Suite*
- George Winston: *December; Autumn; Winter into Spring; Summer*
- Jonathan Cain: *For a Lifetime*
- David Lanz: *Christofori's Dream; Beloved*

231

- Tian: *Shanghai Dream*
- The Kazu Matsui Project: *Tribal Mozart*
- Kevin Kern: *In the Enchanted Garden*
- Yanni: *In My Time*

Guitar

- Earl Klugh: *Late Night Guitar*
- Doyle Dykes: *Gitarre 2000*
- Bruce Becvar: *Forever Blue Sky*
- Stevan Pasero: *Guitar Heartsongs*
- Chris Spheeris: *Eros*
- John Tesh: *Guitar by the Fire*

Cello

- David Darling: *Eight String Religion*
- Michael Hoppe and Martin Tillmann: *The Poet: Romances for Cello*

Flute

- Michael Hoppe and Tim Wheater: *The Dreamer; The Yearning*
- R. Carlos Nakai: *Spirit Wind*
- R. Carlos Nakai and Nawang Khechog: *Winds of Devotion*
- Douglas Spotted Eagle: *Closer to Far Away; Pray*

Classical

- Felix Mendelssohn: *Italian Symphony*
- Peter Ilyich Tchaikovsky: *The Best of Tchaikovsky*
- Edvard Grieg: *Peer Gynt*
- Wolfgang Amadeus Mozart: *Symphonies No. 40 & 41; Eine Kleine Nachmusik*
- Ludwig van Beethoven: *The Best of Beethoven*
- Atonín Dvořák: *Slavonic Dances*
- Johann Strauss: *The Blue Danube*
- Samuel Barber: *Adagio*
- Antonio Vivaldi: *The Four Seasons*

Synthesizer

- Jonn Serrie: *And the Stars Go with You*
- Bill Douglas: *Cantilena*
- Ayman: *Doorways*
- James Owen Mathews: *Liquid Strings; Wonders of the Sky*
- Aeoliah: *Love Is in the Wind; Angel Love*

Various Instruments

- Windham Hill: *Summer Solstice; Winter Solstice; Thanksgiving*
- Narada: *The Narada Wilderness Collection; Wisdom of the Wood*
- Adiemus: *Songs of Sanctuary*
- The Taliesin Orchestra: *Orinoco Flow; The Music of Enya*
- David Lanz and Paul Speer: *Desert Vision*
- Secret Garden: *Songs from a Secret Garden; White Stones*
- Real Music Tranquility: *A Real Music Sampler*
- Hearts of Space: *Celtic Twilight*

- Michael Manring: *Unusual Weather*
- Andre Rieu: *Romantic Moments*
- Patrick Bernhardt: *Atlantis Angelis*
- Dan Gibson: *Solitudes Sampler*
- Colorado Creative Music's Acoustic Therapy: *Relaxation*
- Hilary Stagg: *Dream Spiral*
- Rob Whitesides-Woo: *Mountain Light*
- EMB/Virgin: *Scottish Moods*

About the Author

rian Luke Seaward, Ph.D., is a faculty member of the University of Colorado at Boulder and an adjunct professor at the University of Northern Colorado, Greeley. He is executive director of Inspiration Unlimited, a health promotion consulting firm in Boulder. Dr. Seaward is the author of the popular bestsellers, *Stand Like Mountain, Flow Like Water: Reflections on Stress and Human Spirituality; Stressed Is Desserts Spelled Backward* and *Managing Stress: A Creative Journal.*

Throughout his career, Dr. Seaward has cultivated and mastered a profound expertise in the area of stress management, mind-body-spirit healing and human spirituality. His reputation in these areas, as well as in aspects of human consciousness, has earned him accolades at several academic institutions, national and international conferences, workshops and seminars. Today, Brian Luke Seaward is highly respected throughout the international community as an accomplished teacher, consultant, lecturer, author and mentor. Seaward lives in Boulder, Colorado, with his dog, Shasta.

About Inspiration Unlimited

nspiration Unlimited is a health-promotion consulting company offering lectures, seminars, workshops and retreats for personal growth and professional development. Programs are available for conferences, organizations, corporations and businesses facing the challenges and demands of the twenty-first century.

We'd love to hear from you. For more information, please call: (303) 678-9962, e-mail a query to *BLSeaward@compuserve.com*, or write to: Inspiration Unlimited, P.O. Box 18831, Boulder, CO 80308.

Pearls of Wisdom

There are two aspects of life worth paying attention to. One is our actions; the other is the space between our actions.

—DADI JANKI

Code #7230 Paperback • $6.95

A unique gem of a book, overflowing with profound truths that will help you find meaning and understanding in a sometimes difficult world.

This book will guide you to live each day with an open heart.